THE INCREDIBLE

GOD

CYCLE

ARE YOU IN OR OUT?

Live Your Best Life:
From Him, In Him, Through Him, and For Him

JUDY PATTASSERY

Trilogy Christian Publishers
A Wholly Owned Subsidiary of Trinity Broadcasting Network
2442 Michelle Drive
Tustin, CA 92780

For information, address Trilogy Christian Publishing
Rights Department, 2442 Michelle Drive, Tustin, Ca 92780.
Trilogy Christian Publishing/ TBN and colophon are trademarks of Trinity Broadcasting Network.

For information about special discounts for bulk purchases, please contact Trilogy Christian Publishing.

Manufactured in the United States of America

10 9 8 7 6 5 4 3 2 1

Library of Congress Cataloging-in-Publication Data is available.

ISBN 978-1-63769-186-1 (Print Book)
ISBN 978-1-63769-187-8 (ebook)

CONTENTS

HOW IT ALL STARTED

This book is for anyone who has been confused, frustrated, ever questioned your faith, questioned God, questioned your existence, knew there was more to Christianity than what you have experienced, had more questions than answers, and pretended like you had it together or figured it all out.

I have been all of this and a kitchen sink full, trying to make sense of what following Jesus should look like. I am a third-generation believer, a pastor's kid (PK), cradled into sermons, worship music, and was in the church when the doors were open. I was considered an example child and crème of the crop by most who knew me. I loved my status and enjoyed every bit of my acceptance in the church culture.

I thought I knew God, loved Him, and was a good Christian—after all, I have been a speaker, intercessor, Sunday School teacher, worship leader, and served in youth ministry. I had all the impressive badges and titles and topped on my service to God (at least this is what I thought).

My life was shaken up in October of 2011 when my dad (who was a pastor in New Jersey) unexpectedly went into coma overnight due to septic shock from an unusually severe response to a normal bacterial infection—my world started to get disruptive. He was in coma for about four and a half months until he passed away in March 2012. We lost our mom four years earlier than this incident, and my family, including the church family, was not prepared to lose my dad as well.

It was during this tough season of no hope in the natural, while I was visiting my father at the hospital and all alone, God started showing my spiritual state. My dad, if you didn't know about his condition from the outside, looked like he was just taking a pleasant nap and would get up soon. He still had his charming smile and looked very peaceful. His heart, lungs, liver, kidneys were functionally strong, but the bacteria permanently damaged his brain and left him in a comatose "un-functioning" state. I felt a strong conviction that my inner spiritual condition was like my dad's physical condition. Alive and well on the outside but little life on the inside. I was not living in any known sin; in fact, I was in the intercessory prayer team, was part of an all-night prayer team, in the ministry team at my church, so this came as a surprise. I couldn't shake this off; I knew God was drawing me to Himself and getting my attention.

But it wasn't a total surprise either since earlier that year, I got an unusual message from a young girl at my church who had a strong walk with the Lord. She said that she had a dream in which I was sitting at what looked like a banqueting table along with some other folks that was filled with all kinds of incredible food, but I was staring at the food, unable to eat or feed myself. She then saw Jesus coming over and spoon-feeding me as He patiently proceeded to teach me how to use a fork/knife and how to eat. I remember humorously asking her—are you sure you saw me in this dream? I wanted to see if it wasn't someone else who looked like me! I absolutely trusted the messenger; I had a peace with this dream, knew it was from God, and years later, I still couldn't shake it off.

Although I was overwhelmed by Jesus's kindness to sustain my life by feeding me, I was troubled that I was raised in the church, was part of church leadership but didn't know how to eat. What did this mean? I couldn't help but think, did I not know all this food was prepared for me? Was I scared or shy to eat? Did I not know the food was free and I could eat to my heart's content? Did I not have any teeth to chew the food? Was I such an infant in the spirit that needed to be fed?

Staring at my dad's face at the hospital with tears streaming down my face, I put the two and two together and understood what God in His mercy was trying to communicate. I knew it is an invitation of a lifetime to come and sit at the table with Jesus and be taught how to eat and enjoy the table that was prepared for me. I was familiar with the scriptures in Psalm 23:5 that God prepares a table before us in the presence of our enemies (in the middle of our troubles and challenges) and Jesus's invitation in Revelation 3:20 to eat with Him.

I didn't understand what this all meant but knew Jesus was longing to share a meal with me and wanted me to eat what He had prepared. I knew my true understanding of Jesus was limited; I wasn't spiritually strong as I once thought I was. I knew a lot about God and the Bible and was busy in my service to Him but had little revelation or relationship with Him. I didn't realize Jesus has been knocking on the door of my heart for a long time, but I hadn't responded to His knock or opened the door. So, my prayer became, "I am clueless. Teach me to eat, God." My life has never been the same.

Months pass by, and the week of March 5, 2012, I was sitting in the foyer by myself at CareOne nursing facility in New Jersey, where my dad was now in a step-down unit, still on a ventilator, unable to breathe on his own. It was one of my visits to see my father, but little did I know that I would be burying him during this trip. It was nothing short of a miracle that I was even able to go to New Jersey during this week since I was meant to go to Seattle for a work conference that week. It had been months of praying, fighting in faith against all odds with no miracle in sight. CareOne had a beautiful foyer with a grand piano in the corner; I took a break from the hospital room to be in the foyer and to be alone. Surprisingly, there was no one around at that time, and the foyer was quiet. Lost in a whirlwind of thoughts, with all the uncertainties that lay ahead and tired from the four and a half months of battling for my father's life, I felt a strong presence of God in that foyer like I never felt prior to that time. Tears started to stream from my eyes, and I heard a strong voice in my spirit, "If you would give me a chance, I would love to be yours, Father." Later that week, my father passed away, but this question lingered strongly in my spirit. After we buried our dad, I told my sister about this experience, which undoubtedly, I knew was God speaking to me. I was absolutely surprised when she turned around and told me she also heard a similar voice of God with an invitation to become her Father. Over nine years later, that memory still evokes warmth and love of the Father. I have been blown away by how good of a Father He is, and I endearingly call Him "Papa God!" While in the natural, I miss my earthly father dearly, what I have received from the heavenly Father is no match. In all humility, my dad's homegoing was the best thing that happened because I discovered the heart of God in ways I couldn't imagine. If you are reading this book, this invitation is for you as well. He longs to be your Father. He is bigger, better, grander, and approachable than you ever imagined!

Fast forward to 2013; God took us from an Indian church of fifteen years with the most wonderful people who were like family to us to an inner-city church in Atlanta. Although apprehensive of how we would fit into the new church culture, I had high hopes of being a blessing and serving the church and its missions: a great place with numerous serving opportunities in homeless ministries to sex trafficking, addictions, and everything in between. I went with great hope to serve and bless others but realized it was me who was most blessed—for the one that needed to be desperately changed was me.

I was ready to render all my years of ministry experience and realized I had little to nothing to offer to people's brokenness and challenges, let alone relate to any of them. What worked in prior season was not going to work in this season. It is easier to see looking backward how carefully God guided the steps, but at that time, it was nothing but frustrating and defeating. Fast forward—I sensed a strong prompting to step out of "doing" mode, from the busyness of serving to "seeking" God. It was easy in a way because I wasn't very effective in ministry.

This was not exciting since I struggled spending time alone with God. I could pray with like-minded intercessors in all-night prayers and enjoyed every bit of it, but being alone with God for more than twenty-thirty minutes was way less exciting. After all, we went to the inner-city church to serve, not to seek God in a closet by myself. But, as God would have it in His brilliance, for the next seven years, it would be time alone with God with a Bible, a journal, and a pen. It was difficult facing people's questions of how the inner-city ministry was going when it looked like I was on an extended timeout with God.

I have thanked God numerous times for opening my eyes, for giving me the desire and strength to come into His presence and scratch the surface of the wonder of who He is. I realized I did not really know Him at all but knew a whole lot about Him. Moses knew God by His ways (real knowledge) but Israel through His works (only what God did mostly through Moses—a secondhand knowledge) (Psalm 103:7). There is a big difference; the latter will lead you to become disillusioned and bored with God and even disobedience and rebellion. The former leads to life and life abundantly. In His presence, there is fullness of joy, and at His right hand are pleasures forevermore (Psalm 16:11). Jesus is the joy unspeakable and full of glory!

He is worth it. The revelation of Jesus is worth it. A life surrendered to God is worth it now through eternity. We are here for a brief moment for Christ.

Dedicated to Papa God, who cornered me, disrupted my world, pushed me out of my nest, opened my inner eyes and heart to see the greatness of His love for me, for others around me, and for the world. I am forever His grateful daughter! This book is a compilation of what I learned in His pursuit of me. May you take a hold of these truths sooner and earlier than I did!

To my husband of twenty-four years, Jean Pattassery, who asks questions that no one asks and knows how to make everyone laugh. There is no dull moment with you! I'm grateful for the ongoing laughs, for believing in me, holding the fort, and for all your grace and kindness you've shown me! To my two beautiful children, Jessica and Jonathan, you have blessed my life more than you know! Thank you for challenging my inconsistencies and calling them out so I can become more like Him. Being a parent has enabled me to at least scratch the surface of God's extravagant heart towards His children—why everything that matters to us matters to Him. I am grateful to my older sister, Julie Thomas, who had the courage to stab me right in the front many times, challenge my mediocrity and continue to inspire me to rise higher with God. You saw what I couldn't see. Your simple and restful life in God has impacted me more than you know. To my parents (T.C and Annamma Mathew), who have gone to be with the Lord on whose strong shoulders I stand. I am so blessed to have been raised by two humble people with a heart of gold, sincere love, radical generosity, and simple faith—whose lives made Jesus look great more than their preaching.

Why a book? Years ago, if you would have told me I would write, I would have laughed and not believed. What would I even write about? But here we are, at the end of a historic COVID-19 pandemic year 2020, God put an urgency in my spirit to write this book. It's been an unprecedented year with the COVID-19 pandemic resulting in a tragic loss of a large number of lives, the world on a great lockdown, in addition to the racial injustices, civil unrest, and global financial crisis. If anything, this year has taught us with so much shaking, more than ever, we need the unshakeable Jesus to be our foundation, our source, and hope. All other ground is sinking sand, and only Jesus is big enough to hold us together. As we progress towards the end of the ages, darkness is expected to go darker, but the light and the glory of the church will become greater! I believe God has an army rising who are hidden in trenches but emerging to be the light, salt, and carriers of God's presence in their world. It is divine orchestration that you are reading this book. I encourage you to ask the Holy Spirit to open your eyes to receive what you need to from this book.

In my journey with Him, God began speaking to my spirit to make this little life count by living in the incredible God cycle—from Him, in Him, through Him, and for Him! As I read the Bible, I saw this theme everywhere. In

His mercy and kindness, God started us on a God cycle; your life will be greatly blessed as you live each moment in it and finish strong in the God cycle. You were created by God and meant to be living in the 21st century—you came from Him, He designed everything about you, He put you in Christ, but we need to learn to live this life through Christ and for Christ. It doesn't automatically happen—it's a daily choice. Your best life of joy, peace, success, fulfillment of purposes and destiny, adventure, an exceedingly abundant life will only be lived in the God cycle. It's all about Jesus, and apart from Him, we are nothing and can do nothing. I have also included "chicken or the egg" sections to identify gaps that may be hindering your growth and maturity in Christ based on my own struggles. There is nothing more important in this life than to grow up in Christ. This is the only thing that will last and what we will take with us through eternity.

My prayer for you is that you will read this book with your heart and mind open to the Holy Spirit, you will not complicate Christianity, you will truly know your Father, you will know how loved you are, how much He cares for you, how He longs to be everything He has in mind for you. I pray that you will take a hold of His thoughts towards you (thoughts of peace never to harm you), that you will live with a childlike faith and wonder of Him, that you will live a care-free, worry-free, peaceful, restful life, rejoicing in Him, filled with gratitude, leaning on Jesus alone, knowing the One who has called you personally by your name, will accomplish far more than you could ever ask, imagine or think. That you would avoid unnecessary pain and heartaches in life and live this short life on the God cycle armed with the mind of Christ. I pray that you will truly know your God and be strong in Him and do great exploits He has for you (Daniel 11:32).

CHOOSING THE GOOD PORTION—THE ONE THING

I love to brag about my heavenly Father—He is beyond amazing, there is no one who can even come close to Him, a God who relentlessly pursued me all my life when I wasn't even aware or cared to look back at Him, a God who never gave up on me, a God of a million chances, a God who longed for His daughter to know Him, a God who picked me up from 1,000 falls and struggles, a God who prepared and set into motion every moment of every day and wanted me to trust her Father like a much-loved child.

I knew Him as the God of Abraham, Isaac, Jacob, Daniel, David, Esther, Ruth, Peter, John, and the Apostle Paul, but He desperately wanted me to know Him as the "God of Judy." The more my spiritual eyes opened, the more I longed for Him, the more I began to change from the inside, and the lighter I felt. The same Bible, the same scriptures that I had read for decades, started to come alive on the inside. My life with God was no longer a ritual. There is nothing like His presence. I am eternally grateful for my beloved Father, my wonderful Jesus, and for the precious Holy Spirit—it is so humbling to know that the greatest and the most loving forces in the cosmos were pursuing me (an unknown, inconspicuous woman on the earth but well known, highly esteemed and oh so popular in heaven!).

I could finally see why Mary chose to sit at the feet of Jesus in Luke 10. If you ask Mary what was so special about the feet of Jesus, she will say something like:

- I understood how much I need Him.
- Without Him, I am nothing and can do nothing.
- There is no Mary without Jesus.
- Plus, Jesus is so dazzling; who wouldn't want to spend time with *life* Himself?
- Every time I sit with Him, I am energized, I come alive, my worries, cares, and stress seem to melt away.
- The warmth of His love is incomparable. I have no words to explain it, except I pray you would experience this Jesus.
- He has stolen my heart; His nature is rubbing off on me—I am starting to think more like Him and less like I used to think. I cannot trade Him.
- I didn't have to think twice when I anointed Jesus' feet with an expensive perfume made from nard (worth a year's wages)—some saw it as a total waste of money and thought it could have put it to better use like giving to the poor. But their eyes were not opened to see whose feet I got to anoint (John 12:3).
- There is no way I am going to miss out on this opportunity to sit with Jesus. I know this will not sit well with Martha, but I refuse to be distracted with good things when the King of Kings has come into my humble home. I know I have made the best decision, and Jesus will agree with me.

Martha was hoping Jesus would surely reprimand Mary given all the work that needs to be done in a short amount of time to feed Jesus and his hungry disciples—how inconsiderate of Mary to leave Martha with all the grocery shopping and dinner preparations.

In response to Martha's frustration of getting no help from Mary, Jesus basically responds to Martha that in this life, there are many things you can get upset, worried, and hung up about, but Mary discovered and chose the *one* thing in life worth being concerned about (the good portion) and it will *not* be taken from her (Luke 10:41-42, NLT). In the busyness of serving and cooking for Jesus, Martha missed Jesus. While working for Jesus, she became disillusioned, prideful, upset, cynical, and started pointing fingers. Mary, on the other hand, knew the most important thing was to eat from the Living Bread and drink from the Living Water.

I believe Jesus would be saying something like this to Martha:

- Martha, my beloved daughter, it is more important that you receive from Me than attempting to give to me from your emptiness. You don't realize how empty you really are.
- I am not taking sides here and being unfair to you, but I love you enough to let you know that what you are doing isn't working and will never work in my kingdom. You seek my kingdom and my righteousness, and all these lesser things will be added to you.
- Don't be so eager to feed me, Martha; why don't you relax, calm down and eat from me first?

- I did not come to be served, Martha, I came to serve you (Matthew 20:28). You need Me more than I need you.
- Martha—I know this is difficult to comprehend, but I came to wash your feet. "Jesus answered, "Unless I wash you, you have no part with Me [we can have nothing to do with each other]" (John 13:8b AMP).
- Allow me to serve you first, and you will have an abundance of living water to give to others, and that in turn will bless me.

Jesus wasn't against hospitality ministry or serving others—in fact, we are called to stir one another in love and in good deeds. The issue was Martha was operating in Martha's cycle, not in God cycle. She wasn't abiding in Christ and letting Him carry her burdens. She hadn't learned the secret of casting her cares upon this Jesus who was willing and able to help her and give her abundance of His grace and strength. She is synonymous to a brand-new latest version of iPhone that had never been charged—looks great on the outside but powerless, lifeless, and useless without being powered by Jesus.

Neither did Martha realize she was talking to the King of the universe, whose job description was to make things light and easy for her instead of living in heaviness and weariness. I couldn't help but think how the story would have ended if Martha would have simply asked Jesus for help with the dinner. Could He have brought forth a three-course meal out of nothing? Jesus could easily do that, for He created everything from nothing. Could He have asked Martha to bring what she already had in her kitchen no matter how small it was, and He would have multiplied it, so there would have been more than enough food for them and even plenty of leftovers to share with her neighbors? After all, Jesus took five stale loaves and three-day-old unrefrigerated fish, which was stinky and old from all the heat and humidity, but in His hands, it turned into fresh bread and freshly cooked fish. Jesus could have taken food worthy of garbage and made it fresh and best tasting. We will never know what Martha missed, but it is one of my questions for Jesus when I see Him☺.

Jeremiah 12:5 (NLT) says, "If racing against mere men makes you tired, how will you race against horses? If you stumble and fall on open ground, what will you do in the thickets near the Jordan?"

As God's people, we are called to an "impossible" life, especially as we move into the end-time era and as the forces of darkness are contending at higher levels. We are called to race against horses, not against mere men, and face thick undergrowth/jungles of life filled with uncertainties. We will get tired, exhausted, and discouraged if we are living on our own cycle and can only run this race successfully if we learn to operate in the God cycle. "Marys" can leap over a wall and run against a troop because they are connected to Jesus. I believe "Marys" will outdo and outrun "Marthas" any day because Mary has access to supernatural power, wisdom, provisions, know-how, grace, and strength through Christ that "Marthas" don't.

I love that Mary got to know a part of Jesus that Martha sadly never experienced. In John 11, as Jesus is coming to Bethany four days after Lazarus's death, He personally only asks for Mary ("the teacher is here and asking for you") even before He asked where Lazarus was buried. When Jesus sees Mary sobbing, He becomes deeply moved and troubled in the spirit [to the point of anger at the sorrow caused by death]

(John 11:33-35, AMP). Jesus wept, was emotionally moved, and immediately went into action to raise Lazarus when He saw Mary sobbing. People thought it was Lazarus's death that deeply moved Jesus, when in fact, it was Mary's tears. The one who received from Jesus and sat at His feet could move the King of the universe with her tears. I believe Mary operated at a high level in the spirit and was a very powerful woman, all because she knew she was nothing without Jesus. Jesus was her life. She was able to break the expensive jar of perfume at His feet not to earn something from Jesus or get praised or to seek attention, but it came from the abundance of heart of a woman who received so much from Jesus.

Although I always thought of myself as a Mary because I liked to pray, I discovered my inner life looked much like Martha.

Apostle Paul who was highly successful in this life, beautifully sums up how he worked living on the God cycle in 1 Corinthians 15:10 (NLT), "But whatever I am now, it is all because God poured out his special favor on me—and not without results. For I have worked harder than any of the other apostles; yet it was not I but God who was working through me by his grace." I can't say it any better. He wasn't lazy; in fact, he was a very hard worker and what he accomplished is so impressive, but the secret was that he lived under God's grace receiving from God, operating in the God cycle. On the outside, it looked like Apostle Paul was doing all the work, but that was far from the reality; the superpower behind him was Jesus—He was working through Apostle Paul because it was all done by God's grace. His grace towards Apostle Paul was not wasted or was not in vain. Living in the God cycle and under God's grace always brings God-size results.

In this regard, I think it is important to define what success is so you don't come to the end of your life and discover your metrics of success were totally off from what God intended. My simple definition of success is living this short life in the God cycle.

In God's pursuit of me, I discovered what this life was all about, and I remind myself of this truth often because, in the busyness of life, it is all too easy to forget. I wasted time and energy without this revelation. It sums up in simple four little words: *Jesus is your life*. He is more than enough. We don't have what it takes, but be of good cheer, Jesus has it all figured out! This is so powerful and so freeing. We are here to know this astounding Jesus, and as we know Him, we will realize everything else is so insignificant compared to the infinite value of truly knowing Jesus as *your* Lord (not knowing about Him through others or even through Bible stories). He is your life, and He will give you a life that you will absolutely love to live! To know Him practically translates to believing in Him, relying on Him, receiving from Him, resting in Him. It is ceasing from your own labors and resting in the labor of Christ (Hebrews 4) so He can make things happen that you could never make happen on your own.

The goal of knowing Christ is to gain Christ and to become one with Him (Philippians 3:8-9). There is no point in Bible studies and worship services if it is not helping us to become more and more one with Christ. Less reliance on us and more reliance on Christ. It's worse to be puffed up with head knowledge of the Bible without the reality of Jesus. I believe Mary was gaining Christ (living in greater unity with Him) as she intently listened to Him, received from Him, and spent time with Him, which is why Jesus fully backed her up and did not give into Martha's demands although it was humanly a reasonable request.

Your short life on the earth and eternity will be based on how much of Christ you have gained, the level of your oneness with Him, the degree of Christlike nature in you, and everything that was automatically accomplished because of Christ that was formed in you. It comes down to: did you live this life in or out of God cycle?

Apostle Paul had a powerful revelation of this, and he lived it out as a great example for us, and I believe this is what he would be saying (based on Philippians 3:5-10):

- I thought I knew it all and was working for God until I encountered this Jesus—my background, history, and achievements are far more impressive than most of you.
- I took great pride in them and thought this was life until I got a revelation of what Christ has done and who He is.
- Considering this resurrected Jesus and who I am in Him, I consider all this worthless when compared to the infinite value of knowing Christ Jesus, *my* Lord.
- Because of this Jesus, who is so humble, yet larger than the universe that the highest of the heavens cannot contain Him, I have redefined my priorities, my focus, and determined what will be important to me.
- You cannot know what I know about Christ and not have a paradigm shift.
- I found the pearl of the highest prize in the whole universe—my Lord Jesus, and now He has become the new benchmark to which I compare everything else.

THE INCREDIBLE GOD CYCLE

- What I considered to be significant doesn't even hold a candle to the Son of God.
- This Jesus has extended to me (the worst of sinners, a former Christian terrorist) an invitation to know Him and gain Him—this was an easy decision; I jumped on this invitation discarding everything else and counting it all as garbage if I could just gain Him.
- I discarded trying to be in right with God based on my obedience and my efforts; instead, I received my righteousness through my faith in Christ. Even though I had a terrible past and not proud of it, I know I stand holy and righteous because of my faith in Christ and the righteousness that was credited to me through Christ. What an amazing transaction!
- I want to know this Jesus in every way possible—to experience His mighty resurrection power in me. I welcome even suffering if I can share in His death. I don't want to miss any opportunity to know Him.
- I am pressing on to possess the perfection for which Jesus first possessed me. I haven't achieved it, and I am still growing in it.
- I have decided to forget the past—I certainly don't want to be stuck in my bad past, along with all the regrets of hurting and killing God's people.
- I look forward to what lies ahead—I press on to reach the end of my race. I have learned to keep my eyes on Jesus, live undistracted, and focused to receive the heavenly prize.
- I have decided to choose the good portion, the *one* thing that matters—Christ Jesus my Lord.

We are here to receive from Jesus and gain Him so the hurting world can get a taste of the Living Water through us. If we make this life about anything else, like Martha, we can come so close to Jesus, even serve Him, and talk to Him but miss the whole point. There is only *one* thing necessary or worthy of being concerned about—it is Jesus! Everything else you need in this life is of lesser value and will be abundantly supplied through Him.

EVERYTHING IS RIGHT, AND EVERYTHING IS WRONG ABOUT YOU

Looking back, this scary scripture fitted me well from Revelation 3:17-19 (NLT):

> You say, "I am rich. I have everything I want. I don't need a thing!" And you don't realize that you are wretched and miserable and poor and blind and naked. So, I advise you to buy gold from me—gold that has been purified by fire. Then you will be rich. Also, buy white garments from me so you will not be shamed by your nakedness, and ointment for your eyes so you will be able to see. I correct and discipline everyone I love. So be diligent and turn from your indifference.

This is the Laodicean church—church of the cold nor hot, church of the indifferent, church of the miserable and the poor, church of the status quo, church of the blind and naked.

In our old sin nature, everything is wrong about us; we are wretched, miserable, poor, blind, and naked, basically bankrupt in every way. This is all of humanity's starting point, but this precious church is still living in the old nature. Jeremiah 17:9 (NLT) says: "The human heart is the most deceitful of all things, and desperately wicked. Who really knows how bad it is?" Our old nature is hostile to God and can never submit to God. You can do a lot of good with the old nature, but nothing of God can ever come out of it even if we tried our best.

Apostle Paul talks about the old sinful nature in Romans 7:18-25 (NLT) and tells us that the only antidote to this corrupt sin nature is Christ and living in the new nature He gave us: "And I know that nothing good lives in me, that is, in my sinful nature. I want to do what is right, but I can't. I want to do what is good, but I don't. I don't want to do what is wrong, but I do it anyway. But if I do what I don't want to do, I am not really the one doing wrong; it is sin living in me that does it. I have discovered this principle of life—that when I want to do what is right, I inevitably do what is wrong. I love God's law with all my heart. But there is another power within me that is at war with my mind. This power makes me a slave to the sin that is still within me. Oh, what a miserable person I am! Who will free me from this life that is dominated by sin and death? Thank God! The answer is in Jesus Christ our Lord."

Interestingly, what God saw in the Laodicean church is quite contrary to how they saw themselves. This is like someone eating salads every day, runs five days a week, gets good sleep, they are physically fit, feels great with no symptoms, but their biopsy report comes back as stage four terminal cancer. There is a major disconnect; this church is blinded and unable to discern its current state. I don't think this church was living in any major sins; if so, they would have picked up on their real condition.

I believe this is a church of "Marthas"! A church of the self-righteous much like the Pharisees of Jesus's day who were unable to trust solely in Jesus from start to finish, they failed to depend on God's righteousness to produce righteous living and are still operating in their old dead nature full of filth and stench of self-righteousness. It is the worst kind of sin because it blinds us and will not allow us to see our desperate need for Jesus. I talk more about this in later chapters since I was full of this deadly sin.

They did not see the need to receive from the feet of Jesus; therefore, they did not grow up in Christ as they should and remain on the God cycle. They went to church every Sunday, gave their tithes but lived in their own cycle. Jesus was not their life or source of everything. They started with Jesus but didn't learn to continue in Jesus. Their primary issue was their diet and their focus—they did not regularly feed on Jesus or look to Him and, therefore, continued to live in their corrupt old sin nature. You cannot remain wretched, miserable, poor, blind, and naked for too long if you spend quality time with Jesus and receive from Him! They did not make the transition from the old nature to the new nature. Jesus has already clothed us with His robe of righteousness, garment of praise makes us rich in Him, gives us joy for mourning and peace for turmoil. Jesus is the author of *life*, and their condition is opposite to *life* because Jesus was missing!

This is exactly why Jesus killed off our sinful nature in His death (Colossians 2:11). Think of it this way: when Jesus died, your old nature also got beaten, whipped, flogged, crucified, and died. Therefore, it is illegal for a child of God to continue living by the dead corrupted nature. It's like living off a "dead" you that is dysfunctional, stinky, and decayed.

There is no life in it. It is confusion and chaos when the "dead" is in charge.

It is difficult to diagnose the symptoms because, on the surface, we appear to have it all and know it all. Both are deadly anti-growth factors. There is enough of "good" to get by and survive this life, and it causes us to keep Jesus segregated for Sundays, Bible studies and pull Him when we need Him. In my case, I had a great upbringing, great family, good environment, good education, good job, good church community, and the list of "good" goes on. But good can be the enemy of God. We manage to live through our disabilities and deficiencies and, over time, developed a system to make it work. We learn to wear our masks well and have become masterful actors and actresses. The problem is Jesus is not your *life*, and you are not alive on the inside because you are still living in the old dead nature.

"They will act religious, but they will reject the power that could make them godly" (2 Timothy 3:5, NLT). There is no power to overcome, no power to forgive, no power to keep our hearts unoffended, no power to love our enemies, no power to bless those who mistreat us, no power to heal the sick, and no power to meaningfully impact a hurting world. This is not okay when Jesus paid a huge price to save us from "us." Our salvation is more than a ticket to get out of hell. It is to get us back into a covenant relationship with God. It is to live an abundant life through Christ now and through eternity. It is to reign in this life as a king, a priest, and minister of God with great humility and purity of heart. It is to be a bright light, salt, fragrance of Christ, an epistle to be read—a life of power that looks impossible to live unless there was something out of the ordinary fueling it!

Gospel is not just good news and power of God unto salvation for one day (the day you accepted Christ), but it is good news every single moment until we meet Jesus with power to transform us into our new God nature and power to live freely under God's grace and favor. It is God transforming us from the inside out so the lost world can see a glimpse of who their heavenly Father is. God called us for an impossible, difficult, and a challenging life that can never be done without the fullness of Jesus operating in us. In ignorance, we can live not fully dependent on Jesus and functioning so below what God intended.

We are born with a corrupt flesh, and sin equalizes the child of the greatest pastor or the child of Hitler. No one must teach us to sin—we are born with a double PhD in sinning (anyone who has been around a toddler can relate). We are born into sin because when Adam sinned, sin entered the world. Through one man's (Adam's) offense, death reigned; we became separated from God, and brokenness, selfishness, and pride entered our human DNA.

The moment we said Yes to Jesus and believed in Him, we switched our nature: our old Adamic sin nature was removed and was swapped for the new creation Christ's nature. Our spirit that was dead came alive, but our mind needs transformation to align our attitude/behaviors with our new wonderful nature. This is why I titled this chapter as "Everything is wrong, and everything is right about you." We can live in two opposing realities based on the level of transformation that has happened inside of us and how much we've learned to live in the God cycle.

Below are some of the two completely different natures at work within us. It is important to not feel condemned while reading the list on the left, especially if you are struggling in these areas, it is not just you; it is the universal attribute of the old sinful nature (blame it on your parents, your grandparents, and Adam/Eve😊). The point is, without Christ, our nature is corrupt.

OLD nature—Dead but still operating	NEW nature (Christ) that should be operating:
Where it I get this from? Sin nature that was inherited from Adam and Eve	Incorruptible God's nature and workmanship recreated in Christ (Ephesians 2:10; 2 Corinthians 5:17; James 1:18)
Does a good job pretending to be holy but full of deceit, deception, and corrupted	Nature that is holy, perfect, blameless as Jesus is (Colossians 1:22)
Always having to prove worth and value	Lives proven. Knows there is nothing to prove
Unrighteous: never was and never will be in right standing with God	Eternally recreated to be the righteousness of God in Christ Jesus (2 Corinthians 5:21; Romans 3:22)
Hostile to God, can never submit to God even under best human efforts (essentially an "anti-Christ" nature) (Romans 8:7-8; Colossians 1:21; Romans 5:10)	Eternally in friendship with God (Romans 5:11, NLT), by nature always submitted to God
Can only operate under a spirit of fear (fear of punishment, judgment and torment) (1 John 4:18)—afraid God is not pleased or is mad at them	Fueled by God with a spirit of love, power, and sound mind—perfected in LOVE where there is no fear (2 Timothy 1:7; 1 John 4:18)
Perpetually having to protect yourself (feeling unsafe) and filled with insecurity	Eternally safe and secure because it is God's nature (John 6:39; John 10:28-29; 2 Timothy 1:12; Numbers 23:19)
Filled with despair and hopelessness	Filled with hope with a confident expectation of God's goodness (Romans 5:5; Hebrews 6:18-19; Psalm 27:13; Zechariah 9:12; Psalm 103:5)

Judges God's love and favor based on what's happening to them	They know they cannot be separated from the love of God regardless of circumstances (Romans 8:35-39)
Heart full of lies—> in darkness bearing fruit for death (Romans 7:5; Romans 6:21)	Heart filled with truth—> in the light, governed by life and peace (Romans 8:6b; Romans 8:2; 1 John 1:5-7)
Heart that condemns and accuses and, therefore, lacks confidence in God.	Free from condemnation and accusations (Romans 8:1) and filled with the confidence in God. Lives in the fruit of righteousness: peace and confidence forever (Isaiah 32:17)
Self-driven, self-reliant life	Relies on what Jesus has done and puts no confidence in human effort (Philippians 3:3-4)
Lives trying to cover up nakedness and shame	Unashamed. Lives with power knowing that Christ has already redeemed them from every shame and nakedness and clothed them with His robe of righteousness (Isaiah 61:10). God is the lifter of their heads (Psalm 3:3) and has raised them up in Christ (Ephesians 2:6)
Lives in the earthly realm subject to demonic lies and oppressions	Lives seated in the heavenly places next to the right hand of the Father and beside Jesus subject to truth, peace, and life (Ephesians 2:6; Romans 8:6b)
Lives based on feelings—feels good when doing good and good things are happening and feels bad when doing bad and bad things are happening to them	Ruled by God's thoughts, attitudes, and emotions (the mind of Christ—1 Corinthians 2:16). Trusts in the cross and the power of the blood (Revelation 12:11) to stay undefeated in their emotions

Trying to achieve and work for God's favor and blessing	Rests in the achievement of the overachiever, Jesus, and knows they have been already blessed with every spiritual blessing in Christ (Ephesians 1:3). Believes they are chosen and marked by the Holy Spirit (Ephesians 1:4, 13)
Striving and struggling to be someone, to prove something	Lives in *rest*—ceased from human efforts (Hebrews 4:9-11). Knows that they will never be good enough, holy enough, or perfect on their own. Trusts in Jesus's perfection, holiness, righteousness, and faithfulness to complete the work of grace in them
Like a foolish man, their house ("life") is built on sand (themselves, others, or their circumstances); they stumble on the Rock (Christ) and unable to stand firm. Hears the Word but unable to put it into practice (Matthew 7:26-27). Their life shifts as they shift or people or circumstances around them	Their foundation is Christ. They are like a wise man who builds their house ("life") upon the Rock (Christ)—immovable, unshakeable because of Christ. Hears the Word and puts it into practice (Matthew 7:24-25; 1 Corinthians 15:58)
Soul that magnifies the problems	Soul that is anchored in Christ and makes its boast in the Lord and magnifies the Lord (Hebrews 6:19; 1 Corinthians 1:31; Romans 5:2b; Psalm 34:3; Luke 1:46). Problems are weighed in the light of Jesus, eternity, and the positive results it brings (2 Corinthians 4:17-18)
Ruled by people and situations instead of God. They are threatened by people and have to defend themselves. Striving to get from God, receive acceptance and honor from	They have peace with God and live free (Romans 5:1; 8:1-2). Do not give people or circumstances power to rule over their emotions. Ruled by the honor of God, not

people, and feel good about themselves. Feels hopeless and helpless	people; believes they are precious and honored in His sight (Isaiah 43:4). God is their refuge, fortress, defender, protector, stronghold, strong tower, helper, and deliverer (Psalm 46:1; Psalm 27:1; Psalm 62:5-7; Psalm 40:17b; Psalm 70:5b; Proverbs 18:10; Psalm 18:2; Jeremiah 16:19a; Psalm 91:2)
They look to themselves and their circumstances and end up in despair	They look to God, and His greatness, and their faces are radiant and never covered in shame (Psalm 34:5)
Clueless and ignorant of who they are	They know they are already a "superstar" in Christ and hold the most powerful position on the earth as Christ's radiant and glorious bride (2 Corinthians 11:2; Ephesians 5:27; Revelation 19:7) and live free from what the world considers is important
Ignorant of power and authority that was given to them through Christ. Lives unconnected to their real-life in Christ	They know they have been given *all* power and authority in Christ (Luke 10:19) and use them as the Spirit leads. Knows that every promise of God is YES in God's heart for them through Christ, and they easily say *Amen* to them (2 Corinthians 1:20)
Lives as if you are nothing and have nothing	Believes they are a divine partaker with a heavenly calling /partner of God on the earth (Hebrews 3:1; Hebrews 6:4; 2 Peter 1:4). They submit their bodies as an instrument of righteousness to God (Romans 6:13). God trusts their voice to allow and disallow things

	in the earth realm as directed by the Holy Spirit and knows God fully backs them up on what they say Yes to and what they say *no* to (Matthew 16:19)
By nature, it is unbelieving and filled with doubt	No hindrances to believing and trusting God or His word and promises since they live connected to the vine (Christ) (John 15)
Stuck in the past, unable to let go of the pain or pleasure of the past and move forward	Forgets the past and moves forward in God's promises and future (Philippians 3:13)
Tries to achieve blessings on own strength and efforts. They "make" things happen by own efforts, which can only birth "Ishmaels," causing greater pain	They rest and allow God to make things happen, what they could never make happen in their own ability. They birth God's inheritance for them ("Isaacs") by waiting on the Lord (Isaiah 40:31; 1 Peter 5:6). Lives under God's efforts (God's grace and presence) (Romans 6:14; 2 Peter 1:2; Titus 2:11-12; 2 Corinthians 12:9; Psalm 16:11; Psalm 23:4, 6)
Their contentment is based on external factors	Their joy, peace, and contentment come from the inner life of the Spirit—a life that is evidenced by the fruit of the Spirit (Romans 8:2, 6b; Philippians 4:11; Galatians 5:22-23; Hebrews 13:5; 1 Timothy 6:6; 1 Peter 1:8). They are satisfied in Christ
They live by what they see, hear, touch, taste, and smell (the five senses)	Lives by faith in Christ—uninfluenced by this world (Galatians 2:20)

Worldly titles, possessions, and positions validate their existence—they fall apart without these. They live in a prison of striving and holding on to things of this world	They know they are an heir of God and a co-heir with Christ (Romans 8:17). They know they already have the greatest titles and the most powerful positioning in the universe *in Christ* (1 Corinthians 3:21-23). There is nothing to prove since they are already proven in Christ—they live free
Driven by the cares of this world, deceitfulness of riches, and desires for other things in life (Mark 4:19)	Driven by Christ. They know *all* their needs are supplied according to the endless treasures in Christ, and this world is not their home (Philippians 4:19; 2 Corinthians 9:8; 1 John 2:15-17; John 17:16)
Unable to receive from God, therefore, becomes a hoarder. Limited earthly mindset (mind of this world). Unable to freely give or serve. Ungrateful and undiscerning	Acknowledges, celebrates, and lives with gratitude because they know every good thing comes from God (James 1:17). They do not give to gain acceptance from God or people or to feel good about themselves. Able to freely receive from God and freely give to others (Matthew 10:8b)—they are generous with words, deeds, and resources. They carry the DNA of God and are generous like their Father. Unlimited heavenly/ abundance mindset—the mind of Christ (1 Corinthians 2:16)
Focus is on self and what others think. A lot of time and energy is spent to keep others happy	God is their source for everything—they are able to serve people freely without expecting anything in return, and even if they were wronged

Time spent thinking, analyzing, complaining, and talking about this life	Time spent "living" the life God gave them by faith
Ruled by self-righteousness, self-performance, keeping a record of both good and bad in self and others.	Ruled by God's righteousness, humbled by God's amazing grace and kindness towards them.
Lives under the fruit of self-righteousness: I believe Martha was full of it—condemnation, guilt, feeling like a victim, blaming others and themselves, pride, lack of peace, unsatisfied, insecure, lack of vision, envy, jealously, blind (able to see speck in others but not the log in own eye), quick to judge others, but slow to repent	Life filled with the fruit of righteousness that comes only through Christ (Philippians 1:11) and lives abiding in Him (John 15)
Knowledge of God that puffs up	Revelation of God that brings humility
Impatient and gives up too quickly	Can patiently endure with joy / peace and persevere through difficulties
Lives to please themselves and others—both unsuccessfully—double-minded/unstable	Lives to please God and, in turn, is a blessing to people—> lives with single-minded heart and devotion to God (Jeremiah 32:39)
Fears man—lives for people's applauses, approval, and lives to avoid pain	Fears God not man (Isaiah 8:13; Proverbs 29:25)
Stressed, frustrated, and drained	Full of joy and peace
Trying to produce fruit or act like you got it	Fruit is automatic as they abide in Christ (John 15:5)
Unsure of what God thinks of them (is he happy or mad), trying to earn His love and acceptance. Unable to live as God's covenant child	Fully convinced of God's unconditional love, extravagant grace, and the Father's delight, affection, and acceptance of them, and relies on His faithfulness. Knows God is pleased with them because

	of Jesus and is helping them to work out the changes from the inside out (Philippians 2:13) and live from the new nature.
	Believes in God's covenant over them made through the blood of Jesus (knows that God has bound to them by His oath and covenant that cannot be annulled in Christ) (Hebrews 6:16-18)
Feels unqualified to approach the throne room in their sin struggles and stays away from God.	They boldly approach the throne room of grace and receive the grace when they need it most (i.e., when they fail) (Hebrews 4:16).
Hard on themselves in failure and weaknesses—falls easily into condemnation and accusation	Fully trusts in the cross and Christ's accomplishments, not theirs. They give themselves lots of grace to get up, change direction (repent), and move on without falling into guilt and condemnation from the enemy (Romans 8:1, 34; Proverbs 24:16a)
Weary and heavy-laden life (Matthew 11:28). Unable to cast their cares on the Lord and not convinced God really cares for them	Restful life where burdens are light and yoke is easy (Matthew 11:28-30). Able to cast all their burdens on Him because they know and believe that God affectionately cares for them (1 Peter 5:7)
Unable to live in peace and rest of God and easily falls prey to the attacks of the enemy	Believes Jesus came to give them life and life in abundance (John 10:10). Understands the schemes of the enemy and lives under the rest of God (Hebrews 4), putting on the whole armor of God (Ephesians 6:11-17). Knows God is fighting their battles and will work all things together for their

good and for His glory, and the enemy will not have the final say in their lives (Deuteronomy 3:22; Romans 8:28)

I encourage you to read aloud the list on the right and personalize it, so you will learn to believe the truth of your beautiful nature recreated in Christ. Knowing your real nature can also help you detect behaviors and attitudes that are still operating within you, that are contrary to your true nature and address them.

YOU ARE NOT POWERFUL THAN JESUS

Stumbling block: I did not realize that I lived a lot of my life without a real understanding of God's love for me personally. I knew God loved the world, God loved His children, God loved His church, but never fully took hold of His unfaltering personal love for me and where I stood with Him. His unfailing love is the only thing that can quiet our soul (Zephaniah 3:17). Our roots can only grow in the soil of God's love (not in fear or doubt) to keep us strong (Ephesians 3:17). God is love; therefore, to abide in God, we need to learn to abide in His love (1 John 4:16). If your belief about God's love is distorted, expect to be not spiritually strong.

I believe this is one of the primary reasons for the uncommon grit (spiritual toughness) that Apostle Paul exhibited. He had a high level of understanding of God's abundant love and grace poured out on the "worst of all sinners," as he describes himself (1 Timothy 1:14-16). As you can see, he is one of my spiritual heroes—an unstoppable force that nothing or no one could contend with. God's love is the only way we can be made complete on the inside with all the fullness of life and power that comes from God (Ephesians 3:19). We were created to live and thrive under God's love. If you've been raised in church, you've probably heard thousands of times that "God loves you"—it has become more of a cliché with little power of its reality lived out. I think the global church (body of Christ) has a major love deficit—even if we scratched the surface of the width, the length, the height, and depth of the Father's love toward us (Ephesians 3:18), we would respond and live differently. We would love more, worship more, pray more, honor more, forgive more, give more, judge less, criticize less, and gossip less.

A lot of my anxiety issues stemmed from not living fully anchored in this foundational prerequisite of God's love. We cannot even know God without a calm "still" heart (Psalm 46:10). Furthermore, faith doesn't work without a revelation of God's love (Galatians 5:6b). Too many things hinge on this simple but vital truth of God's love. You end up living with a disturbed, anxious heart, unable to fully trust God, and it doesn't take much to rattle your peace, joy, and rest and get you out of God cycle. To live in perfect peace, your mind needs to stay on God, not your challenges, and you can only do this if you fully trust in Him (Isaiah 26:3). You simply won't be able to trust God and live worry-free when you don't believe He is for you, is greatly in love with you, nothing can separate you from His love, and He will never withhold anything good from you (Romans 8:31-32, 35-39; Ephesians 2:4, Ephesians 3:18-19). Sadly, most of us trust our spouse, parents, children, or a best friend more than we trust God, yet God's love is like an infinite ocean compared to the best love from people, which is like a drop. It's a major problem in our walk with God, and you easily become a target for the enemy. May I urge you to take some time to jot down these scriptures and meditate on them day and night until you are 100 percent convinced of God's love for you? Things happen in our lives contrary to what we envisioned, and if our rooting is not in His love, we can become easily discouraged. If you don't understand that you went from nothing to every-thing by your simple faith in Christ, you will live life with broken cisterns that cannot hold water as Jeremiah 2:13 puts it, digging your own cisterns of power, prestige, satisfaction, pleasure, and possessions instead of living from the fountain of living water (Christ).

It is an unproductive cycle when you don't have a reve-lation of God's love, you live leaning on your opinions, your limited understanding—unable to fully involve God in every part of your life, so the crooked paths remain crooked, the mountains remain like mountains (or even get bigger), year after year, instead of living in a path that God has already gone before, leveled and smoothed out for you. Our lives will have trials and troubles, but our burdens and yoke are meant to be easy and light (John 16:33: Matthew 11:30). We are meant to live in a God oiled cycle where we are led by His new covenant of peace and blessings in Christ (Isaiah 54:10; Ezekiel 37:26; Jeremiah 31:31-34; Hebrews 8:7-13; Hebrews 10:16-17). Over the years, I've watched people who walk in great peace, consistent joy, and sleep like a baby regardless of what's happening to them—the key was they believed God truly loved them and affectionately cared for them, and they were secure and strong because of it. I longed to live in this truth and walk consistently in confidence with God. I did not think much of the fear and anxiety that had become part of my personality makeup until God started to challenge me on this.

You see, I could pray bold prayers and connect with God, all the while living with underlying fears and anxious thoughts that I didn't know were hindering spiritual prog-ress. God was so faithful to teach me and show my gaps in understanding of Him. James 1:8 (KJV) states that "A dou-ble-minded man is unstable in all his ways." Life gets harder than it needs to be when you are unstable in *all* your ways. Merriam Webster's dictionary defines double-minded as wavering in mind, undecided and vacillating. It is having opposite views at different times. When I did good, I felt good and had no problems believing I was loved by God, He was smiling at me, and He would answer my prayers. On the contrary, when I failed, I had doubts on where I stood with God and questioned if I am still loved and wasn't fully convinced, He was pleased with me. I was great at repenting and asking God for forgiveness but was poor at walking in victory and triumph.

I struggled with the same insecurities, pride, hurt, victim mindset, self-righteousness year after year, and the list goes on. The following is vital to understand if you want to live as an overcomer in the God cycle. You cannot look to you; instead, look to Jesus. It's the reason why we can have more faith praying for someone else than when we pray for ourselves. It's easier to believe God for someone else's situation than our own situation. You become your own worst critic and end up disqualifying yourself and getting yourself out of the God cycle. This is a trap of the enemy!

Problem (the lie): I was looking to "me" and judged God's heart towards me based on my progress/ report card. I brought God to the level of my experience and treated Him as a mere human being. In my ignorance, I was dishonoring the God I loved.

Solution (the truth): God no longer looks at our report card but only at Jesus's report card. God sees us in Christ; therefore, we need to see ourselves in Christ and turn away from us. Every blessing, every ounce of favor, grace, mercy, compassion, breakthrough, answered prayers, provisions, protection, and security is only because of Jesus. There is nothing we receive apart from Jesus. If God graded us on our own without Christ, we would have already been consumed and died. Jesus is so significant and powerful, and it is humbling to know that we are in this Christ and His spirit is in us. Jesus is the superstar of all superstars, and you became a superstar in Him and exist for Him.

In this context, I also wanted to caution you not to depend on your forefathers for your righteousness and seeing them as the source of your blessings even if they were wonderful warriors of God and achieved great things for God. This is prominent in some of the Asian cultures where I come from, where family is so important, and there is a great honor given to forefathers who lived righteously, and we can unknowingly take on the identity of our family and trust in them more than Christ. I am honored to have been birthed into such a family and so grateful for all the generational blessings and the legacy that was passed on to me, pointing me to Christ. But who they were and what they did was only because of God's grace. In our good intentions to honor our forefathers, we should be careful not to idolize them or put our trust in their good works to get something from God or have a sense of entitlement. The source of all our blessing is God, and the only channel we receive is through Christ. In fact, we are already blessed with every spiritual blessing in Christ Jesus (Ephesians 1:3). There is nothing missing in our blessing package in Christ. I love that the cross is the greatest equalizer; it doesn't matter if your ancestors were murderers or missionaries; we are equally blessed in Christ.

We are complete in Christ (Colossians 2:10); it doesn't matter how good your parents were or what a mess they were, you are complete in Christ. No one can add to it or take away from your completeness in Christ. What matters is who your heavenly Father is (He is perfect) and your new DNA in Christ (which is perfect). Our righteousness (right standing with God) comes from Christ alone, and the blessings we have in Christ supersedes any generational blessings or deficits we inherited in the natural. Apostle Paul had no generational inheritance to count on (in fact, he was a Christian terrorist and had an anti-gospel family background) and called himself the "chief of all sinners." God blessed and used Apostle Paul in powerful ways. Timothy, on the other hand, was a third-generation believer, and Apostle Paul refers to the sincere faith he saw in Timothy, which was also in his mother, Eunice and Grandmother Lois—he commends the faith that was transferred through generations (2 Timothy 1:5). God is not a respecter of people. While we highly honor those in our generations who have deeply impacted our lives in the things of God, we should not exalt their righteous living over the source of our righteousness and source of all our blessings, which is Jesus Christ—that would be praising the shadow of a person instead of the person itself, blessing instead of the "Blesser." I do believe God can use us as a facilitator and a catalyst for the next generation and use our life to catapult our families higher in Christ.

Chicken or the egg: The only way to get out of the vicious cycle and have a consistent walk with God in the God cycle and live righteously is to accept and believe Jesus's report card. You and I will never be good enough, perfect enough, do enough to receive His love. We are not that powerful to separate us from Christ's love.

It's not about you; it's all about Jesus. For "you" died and don't exist; "I have been crucified with Christ; it is no longer I who live, but Christ lives in me; and the life which I now live in the flesh I live by faith in the Son of God, who loved me and gave Himself for me" (Galatians 2:20, NKJV). Don't give yourself credit or boast in anything except the cross and the resurrection of Jesus (Galatians 6:14). If you take credit for the good you do and boast in yourself for the good things God allows you to do, the chances are you will struggle to receive grace and mercy from God when you fail. It is part of the self-righteous mindset that is deadly that we need to get rid of.

When you fail, learn to quickly go to the throne room and receive the grace and mercy you need at that moment.

> Inasmuch then as we [believers] have a great High Priest who has [already ascended and] passed through the heavens, Jesus the Son of God, let us hold fast our confession [of faith and cling tenaciously to our absolute trust in Him as Savior]. For we do not have a High Priest who is unable to sympathize *and* understand our weaknesses *and* temptations, but One who has been tempted [knowing exactly how it feels to be human] in every respect as *we are, yet* without [committing any] sin. Therefore let us [with privilege] approach the throne of grace [that is, the throne of God's gracious favor] with confidence *and* without fear, so that we may receive mercy [for our failures] and find [His amazing] grace to help in time of need [an appropriate blessing, coming just at the right moment].
> Hebrews 4:14-16 (AMP)

This is a throne of grace, not a throne of judgment. The problem is that when we fail, the enemy immediately puts thoughts in our head, and we start to receive thoughts like, "you've messed up again, how could you say that or do that, you call yourself a worship leader, you are a mess, you can't do anything right, God's so disappointed with you." The enemy hits us with condemnation and accusation—after all, he is the accuser of the brethren accusing us day and night (Revelation 12:10).

God knew we would need a lot of handholding as we grow and to deal with the enemy's tactics, so He made Jesus to be our great and merciful High Priest who can not only sympathize with us, but for our sake, was tempted in all points as we are, but did not sin. This makes Jesus perfectly qualified to help us. Jesus is not rebuking us in our weaknesses; instead, He wants us to run to Him, and He longs to help us in our weaknesses and transition us to our new nature. The only way to live in the God cycle is to realize you don't have what it takes and simply trust in Jesus's works and His blood and keep running to Him.

Below are some signs that you may be trusting in yourself, your opinions, and not fully in Christ (self-righteous mindset):

1. You lose confidence to come boldly to the throne room of grace when you mess up.
2. You only approach God and His throne of grace when you feel right about yourself.
3. You become your own judge—you decide when and how you qualify with God.
4. You don't see God as the safest place.
5. You feel like a hypocrite and stay away from God and His throne of grace when you mess up.
6. You end up asking forgiveness from God over and over again for the same issue since you are not sure if God really forgave you in the first place.

7. You feel weighed down by your mistakes and struggles and think they are showstoppers and believe it is the reason why you always seem to get the short end of the stick.
8. Your own heart accuses you and condemns you.
9. You don't have a consistent peace with God.
10. You know you need to make changes towards freedom but rather not and continue to live in bondage, given you are more concerned about what people think of you than what God has declared over your life.

Again, this applies to folks like me who sincerely desired to please God and fully trust Him but were not fully able to live a life of victory and triumph and had little spiritual growth. We are commissioned to make disciples of all nations and to become great disciples. You will never be a powerful follower of Christ with the above symptoms lurking in your soul.

There is an old and powerful song that goes like, "Jesus is the answer for the world today, above Him there's no other, Jesus is the way."

Jesus is not only the answer for the world but also the answer to the church. The solution for this hurting world is the church—called to be the light and salt of the world, a city on a hill with glory so bright that cannot be hidden, with Christ in us the hope of glory. Jesus is the perfect solution to our every insecurity, lack of trust, our restlessness, every struggle, every ache and pain of life, and we carry the fullness of this wonderful Jesus. To live in the God cycle, we need to exalt Jesus, lift Him higher than what your mind is telling you, higher than your emotions and feelings, higher than your mistakes and struggles, higher than the mess you've created or other's created, higher than your understanding and opinions. This is part of worshipping Him in spirit and in truth—where your mind comes under the truth of Jesus, where His name gets exalted higher than any other name or things that are trying to dominate you! Our true north must be Christ and Christ alone.

Baseline problem: To fully appreciate what an incredible gift we've been given in Christ, we need to understand our baseline problem. Those of us who grew up in church and never gotten ourselves into big sins often struggle to understand the truth of how wicked and deceitful our hearts truly are. I briefly mentioned of some of this in the initial chapter, but some things are worth repeating. These scriptures tell our story of where we all began:

Isaiah 64:6 (NLT), "We are all infected and impure with sin. When we display our righteous deeds, they are nothing but filthy rags. Like autumn leaves, we wither and fall, and our sins sweep us away like the wind."

Jeremiah 17:9 (NLT), "The human heart is the most deceitful of all things, and desperately wicked. Who really knows how bad it is?"

Jeremiah 13:23b (NLT), "Can a leopard take away its spots? Neither can you start doing good, for you have always done evil."

It is not the level of sin that is the problem, although that can have varying consequences, it is ultimately the condition of our hearts. In our humanity, our hearts are messed up equally—doesn't matter if you are a good person doing good deeds or a serial killer doing horrific deeds. In God's eyes, a good person who never committed any major sins is exactly like a serial murderer or a child molester. We are all like leopards with "sin" spots on us. We cannot cover up our spots with any amount of good. It is in our natural DNA—

we cannot help ourselves; we are born as sinners separated from God. It is not our fault; death and sin reigned over us with one man's (Adam's) offense, and the only way to become uninfected, pure, and untainted is through Jesus. Stealing, murdering, jealously are only symptoms of human nature, but the world's ultimate sin is refusing to believe in Christ (John 16:9)—the only way out of our "spots." We will be judged based on whether or not we believed in Christ—simple as this.

WHOEVER RULES YOUR MIND WINS!

We need to get this simple yet powerful truth deep down into our spirit—when we accepted Christ, our old nature life became non-existent and a new life recreated in Christ started on the inside of us. Second Corinthians 5:17 (NLT), "This means that anyone who belongs to Christ has become a new person. The old life is gone; a new life has begun!" Not understanding this truth will hinder your spiritual progress and take you out of the God cycle. It is the simple things that sometimes hinder progress.

You've probably heard the saying, "Whatever you feed grows." The point is to nurture your new nature and neglect (or abandon) the old nature. What and who you focus on will determine what will grow. In this case, it is easy to focus on what you are *not* instead of focusing on who you are since the former is obvious and "in your face," but the latter must be received by faith. Focusing on what is not working in you will keep you in a cycle of defeat. It doesn't matter if you are still struggling with fear, anxiety, greed, pride, or sexual bondages, it doesn't negate the new life that is in you. These are symptoms of your old archaic nature. You are still a new creation—greatly loved by God. Instead of beating yourself up, understand that a part of you is still living under the old archaic dead nature that is now illegal, and your mind still hasn't gotten a hold of the truth that you are already alive

49

to God through Christ Jesus. The transformation of becoming more like Christ is a process, and the God who began a good work in us will continue His work until our final breath (Philippians 1:6).

Along the same lines, Apostle Paul exhorts us in Romans 6:10-11 (AMP):

> For the death that He died, He died to sin [ending its power and paying the sinner's debt] once and for all; and the life that He lives, He lives to [glorify] God [in unbroken fellowship with Him]. Even so, consider yourselves to be dead to sin [and your relationship to it broken], but alive to God [in unbroken fellowship with Him] in Christ Jesus.

This is a powerful truth: as far as God is concerned, you did what Jesus did. When Jesus died, you died to sin—sin lost its power on you once and for all. When Jesus resurrected, you resurrected, and now you are alive to God, and your fellowship with God cannot be broken. This is how God sees you! Our job is to believe it by faith that we are indeed dead to sin and alive to God all because of Jesus. We went from having a negative balance (in the red) to more than 100 percent in Christ (more than conquerors). Jesus outperformed in our helpless state and settled our bankrupt accounts once and for all. This is too good to be true and can only be received in your spirit, not with your head. Your logical, analytical mind can never understand it. Don't allow any other mental pictures that are contrary to this to be played in your head. It will take you out of the God cycle and into your own cycle of self-righteousness and unworthiness, keeping you stuck in the old archaic nature.

Don't focus on the dead: instead, let the dead nature remain buried in the dirt without power over you. I used to work for an Israel-based company, and during one of my trips, the Lord reminded me that my old nature is buried somewhere in Jerusalem when Jesus died and not to keep digging up what is dead, but to focus on what He was focusing on. Focusing on the "dead" will keep you producing dead works of the flesh while focusing on Jesus and your new life will enable you to overcome this life and produce the wonderful fruit of the Holy Spirit. Instead of keeping tab of our mistakes and asking forgiveness for the same issues over and over again, if we are going to get victory, we need to reckon and settle in our spirit once and for all that our old nature is dead, and our new nature now lives alive to God in Christ Jesus (Romans 6:11).

Internal not External: There is nothing more important to God than we grow up in Christ, that we look and act like a Bride of Christ. After all, God trusted us to be His representatives on the earth. Our actions and attitudes matter to God. Jesus loves His bride without spot or wrinkle (Ephesians 5:27) and glorious. Which bridegroom doesn't? He sanctifies (I like to call it God beautifying and migrating us over from our old nature to our new nature) and cleanses us with the washing of water by the word (Ephesians 5:26) but makes us stronger on the inside by trials. Greater sanctification and growth are vital to our success. Our lives are going to be a mixed bag of trials and blessings—God intended that we grow in Christ so we can endure, persevere, and hold our course victoriously until the end. The more we grow in Christ, the more our burdens and yoke become light and easy, and the more God can steward to us because we are strong on the inside. This means we need to be more growth-centric than problem-centric. As our faith gets tested, we do not want to lose the opportunity to develop more of Christ in us, so God can use the trials for our advancement and advantage and for His glory.

Questions to consider when we face trials is:

- What great exploits (which is a greater revelation of Jesus) can get out of this trial instead of how fast can I get out of it?
- How can I go deeper with God and come out with an additional dose of endurance, grit, perseverance, character, and hope (Romans 5:3-5)?
- What scriptures does God want me to stand on so my new nature can grow and rule instead of worry, fear, jealously, and resentment from my old nature controlling me?
- How do I maximize my return on this trial, so it moves my needle towards becoming more perfect and complete, lacking in nothing (James 1:2-4)?

The point is to make spiritual progress so that our inner life of the Spirit governs our thoughts, emotions, and feelings even when things are far from perfect on the outside.

I like what Apostle Paul says in 2 Corinthians 4:16 (ESV), "So we do not lose heart. Though our outer self is wasting away, our inner self is being renewed day by day." In Romans 8:35-37 (NLT), he goes on to say:

> Can anything ever separate us from Christ's love? Does it mean he no longer loves us if we have trouble or calamity, or are persecuted, or hungry, or destitute, or

in danger, or threatened with death? (As the Scriptures say, "For your sake we are killed every day; we are being slaughtered like sheep.") No, despite all these things, overwhelming victory is ours through Christ, who loved us.

Apostle Paul's problems were massive, it was taking a toll on him externally, but His inner self (in Christ) was getting stronger and stronger day by day (2 Corinthians 4: 8-10, 16). I believe what he is saying is there is no way for anyone to go through what I am going through and still live joyful, peaceful, restful, thankful, rejoicing, and undefeated—it is obvious I am not relying on my own strength, I am operating in the God cycle and tapped into the great power from God. Even in the middle of incredible challenges, he is focused on God, being so productive and fruitful, writing epistles that will impact billions of people years later. It is the internal condition of the spirit that matters, not the external (2 Corinthians 4:7-9, 11, NLT):

- Externally: bodies are dying; internally: spirits are being renewed every day
- Externally: fragile clay jars; internally: carriers of great treasure with light shining inside
- Externally: pressed on every side by troubles; internally: not crushed by them
- Externally: perplexed; internally: not driven to despair
- Externally: hunted down; internally: knows he is never abandoned by God
- Externally: knocked down; internally: not destroyed

- Externally: living under constant danger of death; internally: life of Jesus is evident

The reason why Apostle Paul says he will never give up and was able to successfully endure to the finish line (2 Corinthians 4:15-18, NLT):

- He viewed everything with eternal eyes.
- Because his inner man was strong in the Lord and the power of His might, he lived in heaven's wonderful realities, not governed by earth's problems.
- The things that could not be seen and Jesus were far more real to him than the challenges in the natural.
- He saw the present troubles for what they really are—small, temporary, and short-lived compared to the glory that vastly outweighs them both now and forever.
- He stopped looking at the troubles, and he fixed his eyes on Jesus instead.
- His spiritual eyes were sharper than natural eyes, and the former ruled his emotions.
- He perseveres for the benefit of others and for God's glory (so God's grace can reach more and more people, so there will be great thanksgiving, and God will receive more and more glory).

We need to live for purposes way bigger than our little world with a "larger than life" vision to live in the God cycle, to persevere, and be as highly successful as Apostle Paul to whatever God has called us for. Our real success will always be linked for the benefit of others and will result in God's eternal praise, glory, thanksgiving, and honor.

All things, this includes everything we see and cannot see, both in heaven and on earth, was created through Christ and exist for Christ (Colossians 1:16). This also includes the enemy (thrones, dominions, rulers, and authorities)—even the enemy exists for Christ. I especially like that! God is looking to ensure that whatever the enemy meant for harm is used for our good and for His glory (Genesis 50:20). God will never waste any of the enemy's blows on our lives, but we can waste a great exchange with God if we lack understanding. You don't want to simply get what you want from God but remain unchanged on the inside. It is tragic to have endured so much pain from the enemy and be of no benefit to us, others, and, more importantly, God's glory. Stay away from unnecessary questioning on why the trouble came, it can keep you stuck; draw near to God and allow Him to work it all out. He will direct, counsel, guide and lead you victoriously through every challenge (Psalm 32:8; 1 Corinthians 15:57).

The enemy does a great job of tormenting, accusing, condemning, oppressing, undermining, killing, stealing, and destroying. It is easy for the enemy to devour us when we are not living in the God cycle, unaware of who we are and ignorant of his schemes and tactics. God longs to use the enemy's blow to increase Christ in us, increase LIFE in us, increase our abiding in Christ and teach us to sit in the heavenly places in Christ Jesus where we can live in peace and rest. This way, our inner man is protected and secure from the blows of the enemy and troubles of this life regardless of what happens externally (loss, challenges, injustice, or rejections). God is most interested in making sure our inner self is strong, insulated, and stays protected since our "real life" is the inner life hidden in Christ (Colossians 3:3). If your inner life gets defeated, you are defeated. This is the only thing we will take with us when we depart this earth! At some point in our Christian walk, we should be more interested in our inner man and gaining Christ on the inside than only looking to God to fix all our external problems. For you will only truly enjoy life and live to the fullest in your new nature.

Jesus is after your mind (to transform and renew your thinking to think like Him), and so is the enemy—your mind is the most expensive real estate of your life. It is not your houses or land. Every day, you are deciding intentionally or unintentionally who will control your mind. Living from our new nature is catastrophic to the enemy's plans on the earth. So, he will deflect the truth, keep you under lies and darkness and, make sure you don't make the proper diagnosis and won't let you see a way out because he is after your mind. Expect the enemy to fight hard to keep your mind stuck in the old nature; he will do anything to make sure you are not transformed, and you go to your grave with most of your old nature intact. He is also not afraid of you doing a whole lot of things for God as long as you are still in your old nature.

Sometimes God uses the enemy to get our attention, so He can work on transforming our mind enabling us to live from our newly created nature. When this happens, it is easy to fall into patterns of thinking that God doesn't love us, is mad at us, or we have fallen out of favor with God. Nothing could be far from the truth. God may cause temporary loss and pain with the goal of getting to our mind (to the real you hidden in Christ). Whoever rules your mind wins! Either you will allow God to rule your mind or the devil to rule your mind.

What Satan believes about you: many times, I think Satan is a better believer in God, in His Word, and believes the extraordinary recreated you more than most of us do. The enemy is extremely fearful if you believe in the "real" you (created in Christ) and live that new life. Believers who live in union with Christ are the only threat to the kingdom of darkness on the earth because they can take over what is currently under Satan's dominion for God. He fears the power and the authority of the Church that was given by Christ. He knows the scriptures all too well and believes that Jesus is building His church, and no power of hell can prevail against it (Matthew 16:18). He knows he cannot win against the church, and we have the upper hand through Christ. You would reign in this life if you believed what Satan believed about you.

- Satan fully believes that Christ in you is far above him (Christ in you is far above any ruler or authority or power or leader or anything else), and God put everything under the authority of Christ for our benefit (Ephesians 1:21-22).
- Satan is hoping you will not believe in the incredible greatness of God's power for you. He knows you carry extraordinary power (the same resurrection power that raised Jesus from the dead and highly exalted Him at God's right hand) (Ephesians 1:19-20).
- Satan has no doubt that you are part of Christ's body, and you have been made full and complete by Christ (Ephesians 1:23; Colossians 2:10).
- Satan trembles and shudders in terror of God (James 2:19) and Christ who is in you.
- Satan hopes you don't fully understand that you are God's own masterpiece created in Christ Jesus to do the good things He planned for you long ago (Ephesians 2:10).

57

- Satan fears that God's purpose to showcase His manifold wisdom in its rich variety to all the unseen rulers and authorities of his kingdom will be accomplished through you (Ephesians 3:10).
- Satan knows that if you believe in Jesus, you will do even greater things than Jesus did (John 14:12).
- Satan has no doubt that you have been given authority over him—to tread on serpents and scorpions, and over all the power of the enemy, and nothing shall by any means hurt you (Luke 10:19). He fears the power of your feet to crush him through Christ.
- Satan fully believes in God's word; therefore, he knows that you have been given the keys of the kingdom of heaven, and whatever you bind on earth shall be bound in heaven, and whatever you loose on earth shall be loosed in heaven (Matthew 18:18; Matthew 16:19). He knows Jesus will back up His church and establish His will through us on what will be allowed or disallowed on the earth.
- Satan knows if you ever get established in faith (which comes from Jesus), your faith can move mountains (impossibilities), and nothing will be impossible for you (Matthew 17:20).
- Satan knows if you were to submit/surrender to God (to His word and truth), you can resist him, and he will have no choice but to run away from you (James 4:7).
- Satan understands that signs will accompany those who believe; he knows you have the power to drive his demons out, and your hands can heal the sick because you are in Christ (Mark 16:17-18) and Jesus heals through you.

- Satan trembles that you carry the Resurrection and the Life and the *One* who lives in you has conquered the death and the grave (John 11:25; Revelation 1:18; 2 Timothy 1:10; Colossians 1:27).
- Satan will try his best to make sure you doubt God's unconditional love, God's goodness, and unfailing mercy over you and instead will distract you to pay attention to things that aren't working and judge God's love for you based on what your eyes can see. Refuse to pay attention to his schemes and tactics.

This is *key*! Having doubts about God's love for you and not having a consistent belief system that God loves you will keep you trapped out of the God cycle and will significantly stunt your spiritual growth and thereby limit God's plan and destiny over your life.

FIRE YOURSELF AND HIRE JESUS!

Next time the enemy comes to accuse you, condemn you, or tell you are not worthy or good enough to receive from God, let him know, "I fired myself and hired Jesus." I know Jesus is our life and not for hire, but it would be easy to remember, it's all on Jesus now! This also applies to everyday life—fire yourself in trying to figure it all out in your own strength and wisdom and hire Jesus instead.

We need to fully be anchored in who and whose we are.

EVEN BEFORE YOU WERE BORN (based on Ephesians 1): God lives outside of time, and the lamb (Jesus) was slain before the foundations for the world. Therefore:

- You existed in God's mind eternally.
- You were the focus of God's love and were chosen and loved even before you got here.
- God decided in advance to adopt you into His family.
- In His eyes, you were holy and without fault because He has always seen you in Christ.
- He blessed you with every spiritual blessing in the heavenly realms because you are united with Christ.
- The plan to crucify Jesus as your ultimate payment gave God great pleasure because of the joy of hav-

ing you and aligning you to the perfect picture He has of you.

- He purchased your freedom and forgave your sins.
- He showered His kindness on you, along with all wisdom and understanding.
- Even when you were God's enemy (before you were born again), you were reconciled to Him through the death of his Son. If this is true, Apostle Paul says, how much more, having been reconciled, shall you be saved through His life (Romans 5:10)!

ONCE YOU BELIEVED IN CHRIST (AT THE TIME OF REBIRTH): Even though I conceptually knew what happened when someone is born again, could quote the scriptures, and could preach about it, I did not truly grasp the wonder of the amazing transactions that happened when someone is reborn and becomes a new creation in Christ.

I believe everything that eternally existed in God's mind and already purposed in heaven for you collided in you when you were born again. Everything God had already decided and planned became manifested in you when you believed in Jesus. Because of this, there is great celebration and rejoicing in heaven when one soul comes to Jesus (Luke 15:7, 10). Finally, God's thoughts and intentions birthed on the earth in you—God's perfect plan fulfilled in you through Christ. God is full of joy unspeakable, but He gets super excited and calls a big party when a lost son or a daughter becomes part of His household.

I see salvation (rebirth) as the biggest merger and acquisition in this universe: the gravity of it is simply difficult to understand with our small brains or put into words until we get to heaven.

Holy Spirit who drew you to Christ, took up residence in you, you became a new creation and was sealed by the Holy Spirit (1 Corinthians 3:16; 2 Corinthians 5:17; Ephesians 1:13).

- Our names got written in the book of life, and we are called by a new name (Luke 10:20; Isaiah 62:2)
- Our residence and location moved: to the house of God seated in the heavenly places (Ephesians 2:6)
- Our family changed: to the family of God (from slave to a son/daughter) (Ephesians 1:5; Galatians 4:5-7)
- Our Father changed: no longer under the Father of lies (devil), but we have a glorious Father who loves us dearly (Ephesians 2:2, 4; John 16:27)
- Our new everlasting covenant began: under the new covenant of peace and blessings where God deals with us based on Jesus (Isaiah 54:10; Ezekiel 37:26-28; Jeremiah 31:31-34; Hebrews 8:7-13; Hebrews 10:16-17)
- Our destination changed: from hell to heaven (Philippians 3:20)
- Our realities changed: from death to life (John 5:24; John 6:58)
- Our plans and purposes realigned to match what's in heaven (Ephesians 2:10; Romans 12:1-2) instead of our limited "survival" plans.
- Our marital status changed—betrothed to be married to Christ and our maker became our husband (2 Corinthians 11:2; Romans 7:4 (KJV); Isaiah 54:5)

"But don't rejoice because evil spirits obey you; rejoice because your names are registered in heaven" (Luke 10:20, NLT). This is in the context of the seventy amateur missionaries whom Jesus sent out, and they returned with joy and were elated to report that even the demons obeyed them in Jesus' name. I believe no one had experienced anything like this before, and they were amazed at the authority they had in the name of Jesus. In fact, they made such a dent to the kingdom of darkness that Jesus Himself saw Satan fall like lightning from heaven to the ground (verse 18). This was an over-the-top missions trip! Yet, it is interesting that right after Jesus talks about the supernatural authority given to them over all the power of the enemy and the incredible promise that nothing will harm them (verse 19), He makes this statement in verse 20 to not get elated over their newfound authority or in what was accomplished through them but let the source of your joy be that your names are written in heaven.

I think this is one of the keys to keeping us flourishing in the God cycle—from Him, in Him, through Him, and for Him. Our spirit man can only thrive, grow, and produce fruit by rejoicing in our salvation—which is Christ Himself. Rejoice in what transpired in heaven for you, not by the products of your salvation on the earth. Our spirit (inner) man was created to rejoice, and Jesus is the only pathway to lasting joy and peace!

Jesus was reinforcing that apart from Him, you can do nothing (John 15:5). Demons ran away from them because of Jesus. While we should be extremely grateful and expect great things to be done through us, the source of our joy must consistently be Jesus, who is the source of our authority, our salvation, and what He has accomplished in us!

Let the source of your joy always be that you were chosen, forgiven, cleansed, made perfect, blessed, made completely whole, and made righteous through Jesus—let it never be your ministry, the number of your followers, your positions, possessions, or titles. We thrive and flourish in the God cycle when we rejoice in the God of salvation (1 Peter 1:8-9; Romans 5:1-2; Zechariah 9:9; 1 Samuel 2:1; Psalm 9:14; Psalm 20:5 KJV; Psalm 35:9; Psalm 13:5; Psalm 40:16 KJV; Isaiah 12:2; Isaiah 61:10; Psalm 95:1; Habakkuk 3:18).

Because of Jesus, we can never be separated from God's love. Romans 8:38-39 (NLT): "And I am convinced that nothing can ever separate us from God's love. Neither death nor life, neither angels nor demons, neither our fears for today nor our worries about tomorrow—not even the powers of hell can separate us from God's love."

Your ticket to heaven is Jesus, and your ticket to holy living is also Jesus Christ. Nothing changed from salvation. Every moment, for everything we face, Jesus continues to be our salvation, our answer, our door, our way, our truth, and our life. We learn to abide in His perfection in our new nature and in His perfect record as a co-heir of Christ—living as a co-beneficiary of everything Christ has accomplished for us and as an heir of God through Christ. This is a farfetched blessing we have been given through Christ (Romans 8:17). This should fuel great humility and responsibility that we would be chosen and been given so much in Christ. We will not live careless lives if we truly get a revelation of this. This means as your inner man abides in Christ:

- Jesus's victory becomes your victory
- Jesus's strength and tenacity are yours
- Jesus's perfect performance becomes your performance

- Jesus's power and authority becomes your power and authority
- Jesus's holiness becomes your holiness
- Jesus's mind becomes your mind
- Jesus's perfect obedience and faithfulness to God becomes your obedience and faithfulness
- Jesus's success as the highly exalted *One* is your success
- Jesus's humility becomes your humility

There is more, but you get the point. We live and operate from this place as we learn to abide in Christ—we begin where Jesus (our elder Brother) ended. We live where Jesus finished—seated at the place of highest honor in heaven. We fight the good fight of faith from Jesus's victory for us, from God's righteousness that was freely given to us, from His rest where He anticipated and pre-arranged everything we need, from Jesus's holiness, from Jesus's obedience and Jesus's amazing accomplishments on our behalf. We don't live in false humility and performances trying to be something and prove something we can never be or will never be enough. We live feeding on everything Jesus is.

Because we are supernatural—natural combo beings in Christ, every challenge we face is against the rulers, authorities, the powers of this dark world, and the spiritual forces of evil in the heavenly realms and is not against flesh and blood (it's not with your boss, your family, your health, or your finances) (Ephesians 6:12). The enemy cannot touch your inner man recreated in Christ, and this is your power source and what is he after—you can only be strong in the Lord (drawing your strength from Him and being empowered through your union with Him) and in His mighty power (not in your strength, performance, or non-performance)

(Ephesians 6:10). You fight by faith in Christ and through Christ from a place of rest. You put on the full armor of God to protect your most prized asset (your inner man), so you can take your stand against the devil's schemes. You stand firm with the belt of truth, which is Jesus Himself, with a breastplate of God's righteousness, not yours, with a shield of faith in Christ alone, with the sword of the word of God and shoes that come from the gospel of peace not a gospel of confusion or chaos (Ephesians 6:11-17). Every piece of our armor points us to Jesus!

THINKING LIKE JESUS

We are called to reciprocate what God is doing—to be imitators of God as beloved children (Ephesians 5:1). Every child picks up and imitates their parents—they learn good or bad from their earthly parents. This is even more true of our inner spirit life. So, how much are you picking up from your heavenly Father? If you are ignorant of what God is doing, saying, or thinking about you, you will end up imitating the wrong "gods." You will listen to the wrong voices, make wrong decisions, come to the wrong conclusion, and live a defeated, self-centered life. Your fruit and life will reflect the level of your personal revelation of God.

- God rejoices over you with gladness and singing and takes great delight in you (Zephaniah 3:17). You are not going to fully rejoice in God and reciprocate if you are unsure that He is rejoicing over you. You will sing the most powerful songs of worship to God when you truly take a hold of the songs that He is singing over you. So, what lyrics are you listening to? Is it your own lyrics, the enemy's, somebody else's, or God's lyrics over you? This is not a suggestion; God is asking us to rejoice in Him, always and again and again (Philippians 4:4). Our inner man was created to thrive by rejoicing in Him. Spend time in His presence until you come to the end of yourself (old nature) and your ears start to hear God's songs and lyrics over you. In Isaiah 50:4, God promised us that He will awaken us morning by morning—awaken us for what? He awakens our ears to listen to Him as one who is taught. I like this! It is God's job to calibrate our ears to listen so we can be taught—for we are all born with an unteachable spirit. I believe one of the ways He teaches us is by tuning our ears to His singing, His lyrics, His rejoicing over us. Especially for those of us who have been in church all our lives, there is no quick fix—this is God calibrating us day by day, at every sunrise, little by little with His word and in His presence. If you are not receiving *life* in God's presence (fullness of joy, peace, and rest) and become bored like I did, know that your eyes, ears, and hearts aren't fully calibrated to Him. Don't say it doesn't work and give up too quickly. God gives us a listening ear to teach us first—it is one of the most powerful blessings you can walk in! He teaches us first before letting us teach others. Don't put the cart before the horse; it won't go too far. May God give you a desire for things that will outlast the next fifty years of your life on earth.

- We love because He first loved us. If you don't know your heavenly Father loves you, you won't be able to love yourself, love God, or love others. This is one of the ways we lay a hold of (apprehend or "catch") what God has apprehended us for (Philippians 3:12).
- We honor others because we believe how precious and honored we are (Isaiah 43:4).

- We can keep no record of the wrong of others because we believe and are grateful that God keeps no record of our wrongs (Hebrews 8:12; Hebrews 10:17; Colossians 2:13-15; Jeremiah 31:34; Psalm 103:12; Micah 7:19). You can treat people despite how they treated you, even if you cannot forget what they did to you. By doing so, you capture and catch the unconditional grace of our Lord Jesus— the undeserving favor and kindness by which He first loved you and not catch resentment and bitterness. We build our immunity against all the negative forces of this life with a revelation of Jesus!

- We can love our enemies because we believe we were the worst enemy of His, and He loved us, gave Himself for us, and has freely given us all things (1 John 4:19; Romans 5:8; Ephesians 5:2; Titus 2:14). We overcome evil with good (Romans 12:21) because we "catch" that God has only been good to us.

- You can only have peace with God and peace with others if you know and believe that God has peace with you (Romans 5:1; Colossians 1:20).

- We learn to be humble because we see our Lord Jesus as a humble servant who took on the lowliest position for us (Philippians 2:5-8).

- You refuse to live in fear and anxieties because God is perfect love, and He has no fear or concerns about your future and affectionately cares for you (Matthew 6:25-34; 1 Peter 5:7; 1 John 4:18).

- You don't need to live in frustration and stress because God has a perfect plan for your life that was set into motion before you were born; He already took every challenge and complication into consideration and knows exactly how to plant you and establish you. Have you apprehended Christ enough to walk in peace and rest?

- We can live free from the cares of this world because we believe God has detached us from this world with all its negative influences and attached us to Him. We are insulated in Christ. But how free are you from this world?

- We live righteous because God is righteous, and He has made us righteous and holy in Christ. I hope you get the point—you will always rise to live at the level of your personal revelation and expectation of your God. Even if no one believes in you and sees any potential, God holds you responsible to believe in yourself because God believes in you.

- We can bless others because we believe God has already blessed us with every spiritual blessing, and He lavished us with such great love (Ephesians 1:3; 1 John 3:1).

- We can give because we believe God radically gave to us and is a generous giver (John 3:16; Romans 8:32). This is regardless of what you have in your bank account. If you wait for money to arrive in your bank account to give, you will miss out on an opportunity to apprehend a God who is generous. You will see God as limited and "not enough" instead of an abundantly unlimited God. How big is the God you have apprehended?

- If you see that God through Christ has already reconciled you, you will also see that God has reconciled the world to Himself and desires every lost soul to be saved (2 Corinthians 5:18-20; Colossians 1:19-20; 2 Peter 3:9). You will live without judging others and see them through the eyes of reconciliation—if He saved you, He longs to save others. You become an agent of reconciliation instead of an agent of judgment. If you see a woman working the streets, have you "caught" Jesus enough to see her through Jesus? Could she be the next Mary Magdalene? If you see a crooked businessman, could he be the next Zacchaeus that heaven is after? If you see a woman with a history of multiple divorces and moral failings, could she be the next Samaritan woman? If you see a Christian terrorist with anti-God ideologies, could he/she be the next Apostle Paul? Have you apprehended (captured) Christ to see the lost world in Him, or are you seeing people through your own un-regenerated mind? Have you apprehended the God who leaves the ninety-nine righteous ones to get to one lost child? Or are you writing people off based on the level of their sinfulness, their ethnicity, background, and their upbringing? I believe this will be the key that unlocks the great revival and outpouring of the Holy Spirit and the transformation of society. The world has seen enough of "us," and no one is impressed with most of us. There is not enough reality of Jesus in us. They are ready to see the sons and daughters who have "caught" Christ. I am one of His daughters who I got tired of seeing Christ in the Bible and seeing the lack of fruit of my own life to start praying—"God do whatever it takes so I take a hold of you—don't let me get away without a proper revelation of you and the way you deserved to be 'caught.'" I am still learning and can't stop because Jesus is so worthy of this. If you are sincere, God will meet you, and Jesus is worth it all.

Spoiler alert: if you are ignorant of what God apprehended you with, you will not live in the God cycle.

I love the fact that everything about God is extravagant, over the top, and big for His children. He could have loved us with limitations, but instead, He loves us with an everlasting love, and His love for us reaches the heavens (Jeremiah 31:3; Psalm 108:4). He doesn't give us limited mercy or faithfulness but instead gives us unfailing mercy and faithfulness that reaches to the skies (2 Chronicles 5:13b; Lamentations 3:22-23; Psalm 108:4; Psalm 36:5). He is not satisfied to just give us life but wants us to have life in abundance (full and overflowing) (John 10:10). He gives us unlimited strength to crush an army and to leap over a wall (Psalm 18:29). He gives wisdom liberally without reproach (James 1:5).

As you give, God loves to see that you receive good measure, pressed down, shaken together, and running over right in your lap (Luke 6:38) without you having to chase after it. He delights to see our cup running over (Psalm 23:5). He wants us to receive abundance of His grace (Romans 5:17). He doesn't give us barely enough compassion but is moved and full of compassion that never fails (Lamentations 3:22; Matthew 9:36; Matthew 14:14; Matthew 15:32; Mark 6:34). There is no one as generous as our God! We get to become like Him and become containers of living water with a vision beyond the cares and troubles of this life!

Your spirit-mind (new nature) was created to have the mind of Christ (1 Corinthians 2:16). This is not just positive thinking; this is Christ thinking. Allow me to speak from my experience. If you don't get the above apprehended, you will unnecessarily stumble and struggle through life. Those of us who were raised in churches can especially live with categories of sin and don't consider living under stress, worry, fear, frustration, not rejoicing, not fully trusting God, dissatisfied,

THE INCREDIBLE GOD CYCLE

ungrateful, discontent, doubtful, and unbelief as sinful. Do you know that sin of unbelief and doubt kept the Israelites from entering the promised land and walking in God's ways (Hebrews 3:7-11, 19; Hebrews 4:2-3; Psalm 78:22, 41; Psalm 95:9-11; Numbers 14)? But, let's call it what it is, so we can walk in freedom—these are *sins* because your life reflects something that is not of God, and it's not okay. Every sin is an indication that you are living from the wrong nature (the old dead nature) instead of your new nature. I excused myself from this for so many years until I saw that fear and not catching a revelation of the Master is what got the man who buried his one talent in the parable of talents into deep trouble (Matthew 25:14-30). He did not apprehend ("catch") the Master properly—look at what this servant says (Matthew 25:24b, 25, ESV), "Master, I knew you to be a hard man, reaping where you did not sow, and gathering where you scattered no seed, so I was afraid, and I went and hid your talent or minas in the ground. Here, you have what is yours."

The Master's response is rough,

> You wicked and slothful servant! You knew that I reap where I have not sown and gather where I scattered no seed? Then you ought to have invested my money with the bankers, and at my coming, I should have received what was my own with interest. And cast the worthless servant into the outer darkness. In that place, there will be weeping and gnashing of teeth.
> Matthew 25:26b-27, 30 (ESV)

What? Incorrect revelation of the Master (you are a hard man who doesn't operate like what I am used to) bred fear and hiding of his talent in the ground—he puts talents (minas) in the ground (ground is for planting seeds, not for minas/money). He lost his judgment and discernment and became worthless because of fear and an inaccurate revelation of the Master (latter will result in fear). This will cost you dearly to lose even the little of what you have and be given to the one who had the most (ten talents). I don't believe this is talking about your eternal security—salvation is not based on how you managed your talent and your life; it will always be because of our faith in Jesus. He is the only way to the Father, and your eternity is secure in Him if you have fully put your trust in Jesus. This is referring to how well you worked out your salvation, how much of the new nature became your reality, how much of God you actually "caught" a hold of.

I see some resemblance between this servant and Jonah, who gets greatly upset with God when he does not see God follow through on His actions about Nineveh, a people group he could care less about (after all, they were unjust to God's precious people, with generational racial tensions). Jonah strongly reacts,

> So he complained to the LORD about it: "Didn't I say before I left home that you would do this, LORD? That is why I ran away to Tarshish! I knew that you are a merciful and compassionate God, slow to get angry and filled with unfailing love. You are eager to turn back from destroying people. Just kill me now, LORD! I'd rather be dead than alive if what I predicted will not happen.
>
> Jonah 4:1-3 (NLT)

An inaccurate revelation of God in Jonah's case leads to pride and suicidal ideation; he is basically saying, "you made me look like a fool, God, because of your eagerness to merciful and compassionate, and you did not back me up as you should have." Jonah made this about his ministry, his reputation, his people and didn't realize he is here to serve God's purposes as a prophet. Then the LORD said to Jonah, "You feel sorry about the plant, though you did nothing to put it there. It came quickly and died quickly. But Nineveh has more than 120,000 people living in spiritual darkness, not to mention all the animals. Shouldn't I feel sorry for such a great city?" (Jonah 4:10-11, NLT). For all you animal lovers, God even cared about the animals! He was looking to manifest His goodness to a people that did not yet know Him even though they did not deserve any of God's mercy and kindness based on their bad history. God is merciful beyond our wildest imagination and desires that none perish.

It is important how we answer this question that Jesus asked Peter: "who do you say I AM" (Matthew 16:15)? The revelation of Jesus will determine your life, decisions, and impact.

If you need to crawl into God's presence to apprehend Jesus of the gospels when you don't feel like it, do that. Be honest and allow God to change your heart. If you must lay aside your pride and go to someone to get prayer or counseling, do that. This is all too important and should be the primary focus of our lives—to apprehend a God who apprehended you, sparing nothing, and gave you *everything* in Christ.

FIRST THINGS FIRST— REJOICE AND REST

Why is our salvation worth such high celebration and exultation?

Our salvation is everything because Jesus is everything; rest is gravy and part of our wonderful package in Christ (blessed with every spiritual blessing). Don't run after your package in Christ. Why? Because it is pointless since we are already fully blessed in Christ—you can't get any more blessed, you can't get any more of Jesus. We all got the same Jesus in us and blessed with the same blessing. But we can only fully live to the extent our old nature remains dead and our new nature created after Christ is formed. As more of Christ is formed in us, more of Christ can get out of us to impact the world.

I believe the biggest fight in this life is Christ being fully developed and formed in your life—all other life battles are indirect battles to stop the biggest threat of Christ forming in you. This is a good fight of faith because of what it produces in us, Jesus living in our heart by faith! This is not self-development but Christ-development. Even the best version of you fully developed in the flesh is still corrupted. The only version worth anything is our recreated new nature in Christ. The Galatian church deviates from Christ being their complete source and Apostle Paul travails in birth pains as noted in Galatians 4:19 (NLT), "Oh, my dear children! I feel as if I'm going through labor pains for you again, and they will continue until Christ is fully developed in your lives." He anguished over this because it is God's significant goal for us.

God longs to unleash the potential and blessings He already put in you; develop the seeds of greatness in you and give you a life that you love to live. It doesn't just happen— it happens as you seek Jesus, His kingdom, and His righteousness, and all the "gravy" will be added to you. You were created to be the head and not the tail, above only and not beneath. This doesn't mean that you will be a CEO of a company, although that could be exactly what God has planned for some of you. This means that you are created to live above the difficulties of this life in Christ, rejoicing and resting in Him, full of hope, full of peace and joy. Jesus is our head, and as you remain under Him, just as the physical body receives and functions by the physical head (and the brain), you will automatically live an overcoming life. More things just happen without you having to even try. Without Jesus as our "head," we become more like a chicken with its head cut off-distracted, frenzied, powerless, and hopeless. Because Jesus is the head of your life, Holy Spirit will show you what to do, what to say, how to pray, how to partner with Him to see the breakthroughs and purposes of God fulfilled in you. In some cases, God might be asking you to thank Him as if your prayers are already answered prayers and keep looking to Him.

We R&R (rejoice and rest) in Christ. There is not much point in rejoicing in God if it does not bring us to rest and causes us to relax in His truths. It doesn't matter how life looks like today: I challenge you to Rejoice and Rest in these eternal, timeless truths of who Jesus is for you:

- Rejoice! As new covenant believers, we are extremely privileged to live in what the old testament saints (like Abraham, Isaac, Jacob, Isaiah, David, Jeremiah) longed to experience.

  But your eyes are privileged, for they see. Delighted are your ears, for they are open to hear all these things. Many prophets and godly people in times past yearned to see these days of miracles that you've been favored to see. They would have given everything to hear the revelation you've been favored to hear. Yet they didn't get to see as much as a glimpse or hear even a whisper.
  Matthew 13:16-17 (TPT)

- Rejoice and rest! Because God gave you such a priceless salvation through Christ when you brought nothing to the table but chains, bondages, filth, oppression, and the stench of sin.
- Rejoice and rest! Because of your salvation, Jesus with you always, even to the end of the age (an incredible unconditional promise of nearness of Christ)—(Matthew 28:20b).
- Rejoice and rest! Because of your salvation, God the Father, Jesus Christ, Holy Spirit, and myriad of angels are on your side. God is for you, and He's got you (Romans 8:31; Hebrews 13:5b, John 14:16-18; Isaiah 52:12; Isaiah 41:10, Psalm 23:4).

- Rejoice and rest! Because of your salvation, God is always in perfect love with you (Ephesians 2:4; 3:18-19; Romans 8:35-39; 1 John 4:18; Jeremiah 31:3).

- Rejoice and rest! Because of your salvation, God does not change His mind about you (James 1:17; Hebrews 13:8; Romans 5:10; Numbers 23:19; 1 Samuel 15:29).

- Rejoice and rest! Because of your salvation, nothing in this present or future world can snatch you out of God's hands and you are eternally safe with Him (John 10:28-29; John 6:37).

- Rejoice and rest! Because of your salvation, the righteousness of God is yours in Christ Jesus (2 Corinthians 5:21). God put all our sins on Jesus so we, in turn, could receive His lavish gift of righteousness. Rejoice that when God looks at us, He sees His righteousness on us and does not deal with us according to our sins but according to Jesus's worth and value.

- Rejoice and rest! We became an heir of God and a co-heir with Christ (Romans 8:17). We are not "gods," but in Christ, God likes us, loves us, and values us the same way as He likes, loves, and values Jesus.

- Rejoice and rest! You are no longer full of darkness but now have the light from the Lord (Ephesians 5:8).

- Rejoice and rest! Because of your salvation, your battles belong to the Lord, and He goes to fighting for you (1 Samuel 17:47; Deuteronomy 20:4; 2 Chronicles 20:15; Exodus 15:3; 2 Chronicles 32:7; Romans 16:20).

THE INCREDIBLE GOD CYCLE

- Rejoice and rest! Because of your salvation, God affectionately cares for you and everything that concerns you now became God's concern (1 Peter 5:7; Psalm 55:22; Psalm 8:4; Matthew 6:30). If it concerns you, it concerns your Father, and He loves to perfect them for you (Psalm 138:8).
- Rejoice and rest! You now belong to God's family and became His rich and glorious inheritance (Ephesians 1:18; 2:19).
- Rejoice and rest! It is your Father's good pleasure to give you the kingdom (Luke 12:32).
- Rejoice and rest! Because of this great salvation, you have a Father who is so faithful, so powerful, so much bigger than anything you face, and more than willing to do things for you. Your Father loves you too much to not align all things according to His great plan and purposes. You can trust in your heavenly Father!
- Rejoice and rest! Even when you are faithless, He remains faithful, for He cannot deny Himself (2 Timothy 2:13).
- Rejoice and rest! Since your Father did not spare even His own Son but gave Him up for you, He will absolutely and graciously give you all things (Romans 8:32). Rejoice and rest in Him instead of striving and struggling, losing peace, and getting into a deprived orphan mindset, especially if it is taking longer or different than you envisioned. Psalm 91:15 says, "When we call out to Him, He will answer us; He will be with us in trouble. He will deliver and honor us." God will always hear us, deliver us, and honor us and make all things beautiful in His time when we keep our eyes on Him

and continue in the God cycle. It is unwise to place your faith in how long you prayed or fasted or gave to God (it will put the focus back on you and lead to disappointments) instead of putting your faith solely in Christ, who is the source of all our blessings. Because of His great love, you can trust God with all the when, how, where, and what.

- Rejoice and rest! You have a beautiful and eternal inheritance reserved in heaven with your name on it—beyond the reach of change, decay, undefiled, and unfading (1 Peter 1:4). We will live with this wonderful Jesus forever and ever! Hallelujah!

There is a lot more, but at least you have some truths to rejoice, rest and relax in God no matter what happens in this life! As you believe and rest in these truths, we create a sacred space in our hearts for Christ to dwell by faith and do His best work. It is His job to take care of us, align things for us, make a way for us and help us run this race well. He will do that in the most amazing ways!

Jesus must be the heart and center of everything; He is the highest cause of celebration—because of what God's wisdom and power have accomplished in you through Jesus Christ. There is no life without Jesus—everything spirals into chaos, disorder and ceases to exist without Him. There is no love, no joy, no peace, no hope, no comfort, no assurance, no heaven, absolutely nothing without Jesus.

Everything else can be shaken, but Jesus, the source of our eternal salvation, can never be shaken, and we have reason to rejoice in Him always and rest in Him. It is the fuel to stay in the God cycle. If you are taking comfort, joy, and assurance in something else (your job, your savings, your education and experience, your ministry, your funders, family, or children)—it is bound to be shaken and is so unreliable. They were never meant to hold you together—if these are your source of strength, you are going to fall apart. Our hope and comfort should be in someone who can withstand everything—Jesus Christ! All other ground is sinking sand. As we rejoice and rest in Christ, there will be lesser assaults from the enemy since he melts in the presence of Jesus; a drop of Jesus's presence will make the enemy to be scattered from your life (Psalm 68:1-2). The enemy won't waste his limited resources on someone who lives hidden in Christ. He will form the weapons and assault you externally, but it will not prosper internally because Jesus in you will overcome every time. He is not afraid of you or how good you've been, but the only one who makes him tremble is Christ in you.

Everything you face, no matter how big the challenge, is already in Christ because you are in Christ. You and your problems are immersed in Christ, but to fully see Jesus in action, we need to hold on to Him alone, detached from the cares of this world, the deceitfulness of riches, and the desire for other things. This is a simple but profound truth. The enemy trembles if you will take a hold of this truth because Christ in you is marvelously breathtaking and powerful!

SIT BACK, RELAX AND ENJOY

Most of my life, I struggled with internal anxiety, fear, worry, and insecurities depending on what I was dealing with, although I appeared to be confident on the outside. These issues morphed to mind racing, difficulty sleeping, overthinking, and over-analyzing situations, including panic attacks at one point. I knew there was a part of my life trapped in these unhealthy patterns of thinking, and it wasn't allowing the fullness of what God intended. Sometimes God allows challenging situations to come our way to expose the things that we have learned to manage overtime but are severely limiting us so He can help us overcome them. God is not into managing our dysfunctions but overcoming them.

It was the beginning of 2020, on my flight to Mumbai (India) from Newark, that God spoke to me about this in a fresh and powerful way. I had been laid off from my job; the project I worked so hard on, even though I saw God's uncommon favors on it, did not meet its final objectives, and the team had to be dissolved—our finances were starting to dip, and all the jobs that I wanted and thought would be a good fit did not pan out. God foreknew everything and knew I would come back from India on one of the last flights before the world came to a standstill with COVID-19, and things would go from bad to worse. I believe we hear God the best in dark times because He knows we need Him to survive. I got a coach ticket to Mumbai, but God gave me a free first-class ticket upgrade on United Airlines from Newark to Mumbai—thanks to my sister, who I was traveling with, who is a United global service member. God works favors for us through others!

I heard God loud and clear as the United Airlines pilot came on the speaker and said the all familiar phrases I've heard a hundred times before and never paid attention to—"Sit back, relax and enjoy your trip—let us know if you need anything to make your trip more comfortable." As I heard these words, tears started to flow from my eyes.

I strongly sensed in my spirit God saying, "I want you to know and believe you are a queen in my kingdom; I want you to kick back, sit back, relax and enjoy your life with a childlike faith. I don't want you to worry about a thing, even for a moment. I am your pilot, the Ancient of Days; I know what I am doing, I know where I am going and how to get you to your destination. Trust my thoughts, my ways, and my plans. I will never fail you. Don't trust in your own faulty opinions. I want you to live like you are seated in first class, where everything you need is provided, and you are fully taken care of." God will speak through anyone and any-thing—don't limit Him to Sunday morning service or a mes-sage. He speaks even through a donkey!

I thoroughly enjoyed that flight to Mumbai—I didn't care we had a couple of hours of delay in Newark. I arrived rested with very little jet lag. I signed a consulting contract while I enjoyed my trip to India. God worked while I rested. This was a big lesson for me in letting go so God can take over. We went there to take care of a land that belonged to my parents—since they died unexpectedly, we did not have proper paperwork or documentation to be able to success-fully transfer the land to us. The bureaucracy and red tapes in India already add multiple layers of complication and our problem made things worse. God gave us such favor that the transfer of titles and deeds were done in less than forty-five minutes. I believe when we worry and live in fear, we unintentionally take control of the situation, and it hinders God from doing His best work. Worry and fear indicate that our old nature is at work, and in a way, God steps out of the way. I used to say Christian clichés like "thank you, Lord, that you are in control" until the Lord pointed out to me that He was not in control as He would like to because my old nature was reigning and taking full control. These were just cute words that made me feel good, but there was no release of control from my heart. You and God cannot be in control at the same time. God is sovereign and rules over us, but I do believe for God to accomplish His full work in us and show Himself off, He needs us to yield ourselves to Him—to come under His mighty hand, His love, His peace, His joy, His grace, His perfect ways, plans, and timing. He honors our free will, and we get to choose how much of Jesus we want— we choose daily to be a Mary or a Martha.

It is important to take time with God to see if there are areas in our hearts that we are unknowingly taking control of and not able to fully release to God, so we can see the breakthroughs that God longs to give us. I realized that I trusted United airlines to take me across the oceans more than I trusted my heavenly Father, and that deeply bothered me. I did not check the airplane, review any quality checks, had no knowledge of the plane's engine performance to see if it met all specifications. I didn't know if the pilot was experienced or knows how to navigate through turbulence or rough patches. I had no problem trusting an American brand name based on the airline's reputation—I believed they did their due diligence, ran all necessary tests and their pilots were trained and experienced. It gave me new prayers to ask God to deal with my trust issues.

God was inviting me to learn to trust and believe in His eternal and unchanging brand names for me—El Shaddai (my God Almighty), El Elyon (My Most High God), Jehovah Nissi (my banner of victory), Jehovah Tsidkenu (The Lord my righteousness), Jehovah Shammah (The Lord is there for me always), Jehovah Rapha (The Lord my healer), Jehovah Shalom (The Lord is peace over me) and Jehovah Jireh (God is my provider).

I learned that we make bad pilots but created in Christ to be great passengers. We are so fickle and clueless, but the enemy will make us believe that we are falsely in control when we don't even have a GPS or know what's going to happen next, where the world is headed to and can't even control our next breath. We think we are doing well sitting in the pilot seat, it feels good to be in "false" control, but we will end up frustrating ourselves and not living in God's fullness. God doesn't give us His full plan; we get to trust Him step by step. When my mind wanders and comes under anxiety, I hear the Lord gently reminding me, "Hey Queen, go back to your first-class cabin and be seated, please. Let me do my job."

I go back to that trip mentally and to the voice I heard in my spirit when my old fears and anxieties try to sneak up on me. I have to remind myself again and again, "Fear and anxiety, you have no place in my heart any longer. I refuse to come under your false voices that appear to blow things out of proportion in my mind. You've played mind games with me for too long. It's not going to work anymore. I am a queen in the kingdom of God. I handed over my worries, cares, and fears to Jesus, so you have to deal with Jesus on this; I am safe and secure in Him." Even though I had a job, my hours began dwindling away, and so did the finances as

COVID-19 hit; the enemy contended hard, life looked so different from what I thought, I was forced to face my fear of not having enough, but God made 2020 the most glorious year for me—God revealed Himself in so many ways! We ended the year beyond my expectation. This book is a result of God showing Himself in ways I could not even fathom. He is absolutely a stunning God—you were born to know Him! Nothing or no one comes close to Him. Expect troubles (we are called for this), but if you stick with God, He will overcome every obstacle, teach you to live in the God cycle, and give you a life worth living.

When I was younger, I used to have this fear that surrendering to God meant a miserable life—God will take you to some remote place in Africa or the third world where there is no running water, no electricity with creepy reptiles, and living in a hut. I sure did not want that. I couldn't sing the beloved hymn from my heart, "I surrender all, All to Thee, my blessed Savior, I surrender all" until I saw some happy missionaries full of the Holy Spirit, full of life and full of joy who have lived in places like the above. It doesn't matter if God called you to work as a CEO in a Fortune 500 company and you live in a penthouse in New York City, or you are a stay-at-home mom or a business owner or a missionary in Africa, you were created for a life you will love to live— in Him, through Him and for Him. "Happy are the people whose God is the Lord" (Psalm 144:15). Happiness is not external; it is based on who is Lord over your life and whether you are living in the God cycle!

WHO IS HOLDING THE STRING TO YOUR HEART?

This is an important question and will determine whether you live your life on the God cycle and your growth in Christ.

We are instructed to throw off (discard) our old sinful nature, the former corrupted way of life that is already crucified and non-existent in Christ and instead put on the new nature, created to be like God—truly righteous and holy (Ephesians 4:22, 24). God wants us to put to death the sinful, earthly things that are still lurking within us (so we are free from impurity, lust, evil desires, greed, love of this world and free from worshipping the stuff of this world) and be renewed as we learn to know our Creator and become like Him (Colossians 3:5-10).

I pray that the next couple of chapters might help you to see what "clothes" from your old corrupted nature closet may be still hanging around that needs to be stripped away, so you think like Jesus and become more like Jesus. Old nature is shaped by things of this world (lust of the flesh, lust of the eye, and pride of life) and driven by our five senses instead of God.

In my spirit, I heard the Lord saying to me once, "You were created to look great and smell great." I knew right away this was referring to the condition of my inner life. The old corrupted nature is plain stinky and ugly. If the old nature is dominating your thought and life, it is not making you look or smell good as God intended. Your life is too precious to live in filthy, raggedy, out of fashion, obsolete, ill-fitting clothes of the old corrupted nature. We would not wear these kinds of clothes in the physical (neither can it be even donated except tossed in the garbage), so why would we live like this in the most important area of our life? In the same scripture, it says this is a reason why the anger of God is coming (Colossians 3:6). We are not under God's wrath by any means since Jesus took that for us, but God is serious when it comes to changing our wardrobes—He will shake things to get our attention to make us look good and smell good. He is making us powerful, productive, influential and useful, no longer powerless and useless. Don't ignore Him.

The enemy is nervous when you start looking great and smelling great—and the only way we look good is by putting on Christ, and the only way to smell good (pleasing aroma of Christ) is by abiding in Christ. In Christ, your new inner self is already draped with a robe of His righteousness and is radiant. Because of Jesus, we can look and smell like resurrection and *life* instead of the stench of death and the grave. God desires us to blossom like the lily, sending roots deep into the soil with its branches spread out like beautiful olive trees and become as fragrant as the cedars in Lebanon (Hosea 14:5b, 6).

If we could spiritually discern the difference between our true beautiful nature versus old corrupted nature, we would not put up with our old nature. We should be far more concerned about our spiritual health and spiritual beauty than our physical health and looks. Apostle Paul weighs both on a scale and says in 1 Timothy 4:8, "For bodily exercise profits a little, but godliness is profitable for all things, having promise of the life that now is and of that which is to come." Our spiritual beauty is far more reaching, rewarding, and impactful now and through eternity. Greater spiritual beauty will make all other areas of life to thrive as God intended.

I believe that all the beautiful accessories that are mentioned in Isaiah 3:18-24 that makes the daughter of Zion beautiful is a depiction of the beauty of the Bride of Christ that comes from a place of abiding in Jesus (in this context, God takes away her beauty because of judgment but because of Jesus, we are forever clothed with His beauty): you as the Bride of Christ was meant to be adorned with ornaments, headbands, crescent necklaces, earrings, bracelets, veils, scarves, ankle bracelets, sashes, perfumes, charms, rings, jewels, party clothes, gowns, capes, purses, mirrors, fine linen garments, head ornaments, shawls, smelling of sweet perfume, wearing a sash, with elegant hair, and rich robes. God splurged you from head to toe with everything in Christ. You have become irresistibly beautiful in Christ!

We are the most stunning and powerful when Jesus is the only *one* holding the string to our heart and our only lifeline. This is your best life-powerful, joyful, peaceful, thankful, and hopeful; everything else will be beautifully aligned in God's ways and timing without you struggling for it. This is the only way our inner life in Christ can remain strong even through the storms of this life. Your inner life was built to last through eternity and can withstand any force, opposition, and stand against Satan and his demonic realms because you are in Christ, but this is only practically achieved by abiding in Christ.

God foreknew all our difficulties and paid a high price to conquer them through Christ. I believe God has a customized package with our name on it to overcome every wound, every hurt, every injustice we have ever gone through. He knows exactly how to heal and bring you in greater freedom with Him. He is our faithful High Priest and the only one who fully understands us and can sympathize and relate with us (Hebrews 2:17; 4:14-15). He is the safest place in this universe.

I suggest you take some time to ponder and ask the Holy Spirit to show you areas in your life that you may be holding on to things other than Jesus. He is so faithful and will help you. The following questions might be helpful with this exercise and may expose some hidden trust issues in your heart to see if there are other strings you have allowed to control your heart:

- Who and what controls your emotions and feelings? Look for people or situations that have the power to control your thoughts and emotions.
- What makes you mad, sad, happy, or feel hurt?
- Who are you trying to keep happy or trying to please?
- What makes you fearful, concerned, and worried?
- What makes you lose sleep?
- Who and what makes you uncomfortable?
- What makes you come alive?

I encourage you to spend some time with God to heal any hurts, offenses, disappointments, or discouragement or deal with any idols of the heart other than God. Let them go and give everything to Jesus. He longs to heal you and give you His peace and joy in exchange. Learn to cast all your cares, hurts, and disappointments on Jesus on a regular basis, so He can be the only string to your heart.

God wants us to be strong and stable people and does not want anyone or anything to have more power and control over our emotions than Him. God wants us to be ruled by Him, not by other people's hurts and pain. We were created to be mentally and emotionally tough as Jesus as we abide in Him in our new nature. If people or situations rule over us, it will ultimately hurt us to our detriment; we can hurt others and limit the abundant life we were created for and hinder what God could have accomplished through us. This is also indirectly idolatry-giving undue attention to anything or anyone more than Jesus. Enjoy people thoroughly, but live free from them so you can remain in the God cycle.

In the early years of God's pursuit of me, He highlighted these beautiful promises in Jeremiah 32:38-41 (NKJV); I didn't appreciate the depth of it even though I read it and prayed for "one heart and one way" many times:

> They shall be My people, and I will be their God; then I will give them one heart and one way, that they may fear Me forever, for the good of them and their children after them. And I will make an everlasting covenant with them, that I will not turn away from doing them good; but I will put My fear in their hearts so that they will not depart from Me. Yes, I will rejoice over them to do them good, and I will assuredly plant them in this land, with all My heart and with all My soul.

In Christ, our inner heart was calibrated to be united with Jesus, one with His heart and one with His way and Christ ruling over our thought life. We avoid a lot of emotional pain when we live yielded to Jesus—the same pain doesn't affect you as much because your inner life is hidden in Christ, and it is insulated. The more you remain dead to your old nature (living crucified with Christ) and the more alive you are to Christ, the less you are hurt and overwhelmed by this life. A dead person in a coffin is not impacted by anyone's praises, criticisms, or by negative situations. Our reactions, responses, and our emotions are a good reflection of what "nature" is ruling us and who is controlling the string of our heart.

In this life, we will not have our way every time; people and circumstances are not going to go the way we want them to go. In this fallen world, we all want our way and believe we are justified and right. God knew this, and His answer was simple yet highly effective—"don't let anyone rule your heart except *Me*." God is the only one who will never leave you, never disappoint you, never fail you, always on your side, and always looking out for your best and working everything out for your good and for His glory. Our hearts can only be protected and secure in Him. God knew everyone, and everything has the potential to fail and disappoint us, so don't give them the precious strings to your heart and allow people to take you out of the God cycle.

This is how it might play itself out in real life:

- After everything I have done, how could you treat me this way? How could you be so ungrateful and unkind?
- After how good and kind I was to you, how could you stab me in the back and be so unjust?
- After bending over backward for you for all these years, how could you not be there for me when I needed you?

- After working so hard all these years at work, are you going to just lay me off?

Are these difficult and painful situations? You bet especially when it is people who are closest to us, but thanks be to Christ, we don't have to live in a "Cause and Effect" zone like the rest of the world. In our old sin nature (flesh), it will always be about us (what we did)—our work, our giving, our efforts, and we will always expect the recipient to give back to us or at least not hurt us based on our goodwill towards them. By doing this, we set up a foundation based on our good deeds, our good behavior (which is nothing but deadly self-righteousness) instead of depending on the righteousness of God, and we can get ourselves into a lot of trouble.

We need to remind ourselves that we do not war against people (flesh and blood), but the real war is against principalities and powers of darkness to get us off God cycle, defeat us and make us powerless. We do this with God too—we give hoping to get back in our timetable; we serve God to get extra credit with Him or get additional favors. When we don't get what we want, when we want, we can get discouraged with God. All of this will cause us to drift away and slide off God cycle where we will live defeated. God has promised to do exceedingly abundantly, but it will be for those who consistently rejoice in the Lord so they can patiently endure through Christ, those who do not become weary in doing good even when they don't feel like it and continue to live joyfully looking to Jesus alone. This will also propel more Jesus to be formed in us—which is our most prized possession in this life. This is the theme of this book—It is living in a "360-degree Jesus" in the God cycle: to see yourself, your past, your present, your future, your dreams, your family, your problems, your health, your friends, your enemies, your ministry, every believer, every unbeliever, the world, anything and everything through Christ. Do whatever it takes for Christ to be formed in you so you can live this short life in an impactful way.

As a parent, I believe this is the best inheritance you can leave for your children—a greater revelation of Jesus inside of you, so you can rise your generational line in Christ and bring greater freedom from generational pressures and mindsets that have tried to hinder spiritual progress and fullness of God to operate in families. Christ has redeemed and set us free us from this faulty old sin nature, so we don't need to continue to pamper and feed this terrible nature of ours. The old nature is utterly flawed that whatever we do is really serving us in the end—its intentions and motivations are always wrong, and feeding this nature will get us out of the God cycle. While we should be grateful for all the blessings that come from people and honor people who have so blessed us, to remain in the God cycle, we will need to abide and rest in Jesus alone. We cannot get or, in some ways, demand from people that only God can give.

No one else died for us; it can be our living water, the bread of life, the great light, the Author of Life, the mighty Savior, or the fairest of ten thousand to our soul. We look to Him for our worth and value; He is our source of joy, our source of satisfaction, and the source of our supply that will never run out. Jesus died so we can walk in complete freedom so we can "freely" give—free from expectations and free from people. It's giving with no strings attached, just like God loves us and gives to us freely with no strings attached. We get to be like our Father. There is a big difference between "giving" and "giving freely." You can only do the latter in and through Christ and once you've learned to receive freely from God.

You were created in Christ to be an eagle—as you abide in Christ, you were designed to rise with wings like an eagle—soaring above the cares and immaterial pursuits of this life. Jesus is the only one who can take us up, giving us supernatural energy to live far above the ground level, undistracted by what's distracting everyone else. We were created to run but not become weary, walk but not grow tired (Isaiah 40:31). Without Jesus, we will remain on the ground as "chickens" disturbed by everything that happens around us. If circumstances and people hold the string to our heart more than Jesus, we are going to become weary (exhausted, fatigued, beat) and tired. It will be mentally, emotionally, physically exhausting while making no spiritual progress. We cannot abide in Christ and others at the same time—it will be one or the other.

"Whoever has no rule over his own spirit is like a city broken down, without walls" (Proverbs 25:28, NKJV). If we allow others or circumstances to control our heart, our inner man/spirit will be weak, like a city broken down with no walls. For no one in their right mind would leave their house with all doors open and walls knocked down with all their precious belongings and valuables inside. Yet, so many of us live this way—vulnerable to the enemy's plunder, killing, and destroying. We cannot win people, cities, and nations for Jesus if our inner spirits are broken and defenseless. We will not be able to withstand the forces of darkness. Our strength is not in our talents, our gifts, our programs, our church buildings, our staff, or our ministries—our strength and power is only to the extent we have learned to abide in Christ and His achievements for us. The former is good and necessary, but without full dependency on Jesus, it will not be fruitful as God intended. "For it is 'Not by might nor by power, but by My Spirit,' says the Lord of hosts" (Zechariah 4:6b, NKJV).

This is all too important, and I don't believe we will fulfill our destinies on the earth and successfully live out our faith with multiple strings hanging from our hearts because the plan of God for your life is only in Christ. "For in Him, we live and move and have our being" (Acts 17:28a, NIV). In Him, we live, we work, we think, we speak, we worship, we pray, we serve. Outside of Jesus, there is no real living or movement.

God loves to see His children happy—which parent doesn't? Every good and perfect gift comes from Him (James 1:17)—He blesses us with family, spouse, children, siblings, parents, church body, education, careers, ministries, businesses, positions, possessions, memorable vacations, and wonderful memories. These are bountiful gifts from our God, who loves to lavish them on us, but they don't have the power or ability or are designed to sustain our lives. Only Jesus can—He is the only one who can meet our deepest needs. We are free to enjoy what God gives us but should not be bound by the gifts that they rule over our life instead of Christ.

We can fully count on God to give us what we need when we need it. But we will end up in frustration if we look to mere humans (yourself and others) and things of this world to deliver what they cannot deliver. "Don't put your trust in mere humans. They are as frail as breath. What good are they?" (Isaiah 2:22, NLT). No one else is that capable or powerful.

How can you top Jesus? He is the greatest of the greatest. No one else comes even remotely close to loving us or caring for us as Jesus does. Let Him be our to-go person in every situation, our life source, our treasure—because you have Him, you already have everything you need. Your future is far too important. Let no one hold strings to your heart except Jesus. Let no one have that kind of power over you except Christ!

LIVING FREE—WHAT CAN WE LEARN FROM KING DAVID?

We don't always live with full awareness of what's going on the inside of us. The following prayer of King David in Psalm 139 follows after his beautiful rendition of twenty-two scriptures of how well God knows him, how God alone knows what he is about to speak, how God reads his mind like an open book, how God has gone into the future to prepare the way, how in His kindness He follows before and behind him and how His hand of love is upon his life and how marvelously and wonderfully God has made him and always thinking about him. David then says:

> God, I invite your searching gaze into my heart. Examine me through and through; find out everything that may be hidden within me. Put me to the test and sift through all my anxious cares. See if there is any path of pain I'm walking on, and lead me back to your glorious, everlasting ways—the path that brings me back to you.
> Psalm 139:23-24 (TPT)

We can easily stumble in paths of pain that lead us away from the path of glorious life. The amplified bible refers to the path of pain as a "wicked or hurtful way" in verse 24. Hurtful way is a wicked way. At any moment, we are choosing to walk in either the everlasting way (God's ways) or wicked/ hurtful way (our ways). For there are only two paths to live this life. It might be a path of pain caused by disappointment, discouragement, other people's dysfunctions, fear, or cares. When we don't exchange life's hurts and cares with God (and live focused on us and others instead of God), we unintentionally stray away from the beautiful path of life, and the fruit of our life will be more like we are walking in wickedness. This is all too important! It is the little leaven that works through the whole batch of dough (Galatians 5:9) and takes us out of sync with God. Your best life is lived under the mighty hand of God (1 Peter 5:6). It is important to know who God is for you, who you are to Him, so you can give your cares to God, live free from hurts, and fight the good fight of faith to stay on the glorious path with Christ. You matter so much to God to live your precious life in any wicked or hurtful way. I encourage you to read Psalm 139, especially when you feel lost and out of sorts, to re-center you back to God.

I love the heart of David in Psalm 142:1-5 (NLT):

> I cry out to the LORD; I plead for the LORD's mercy. I pour out my complaints before him and tell him all my troubles. When I am overwhelmed, you alone know the way I should turn. Wherever I go, my enemies have set traps for me. I look for someone to come and help me, but no one gives me a passing thought!

> No one will help me; no one cares a bit
> what happens to me. Then I pray to you,
> O Lord. I say, "You are my place of ref-
> uge. You are all I really want in life."

David had tremendous wisdom that came from the fear of the Lord even though he messed up and failed many times. After all, he was called by God as the man after His own heart. Below are some additional thoughts to be more in tune with what's happening in our inner life and deal with things as they come up.

- Be open and honest with your feelings to God. David is not afraid to let God know He is feeling insecure, trapped, overlooked, rejected, ignored, frustrated, and over his head.
- The issues of the heart and bad emotions never go away until you receive freedom from Jesus. It starts to manifest and express itself in ungodly ways that will catch you by surprise. Matthew 7:17 (ESV), "So, every healthy tree bears good fruit, but the diseased tree bears bad fruit." We should judge our own lives by our fruit.
- As part of your devotional time with God, set aside time to bring forward your complaints and troubles to God first instead of people. I believe it is one of the reasons why David lived with a free spirit.
- It's important that we practice to "unload" our unhealthy emotions and cares to God, who can do something about it on a daily basis, so we can "load" up on His peace, joy, presence, and benefits. "Blessed be the Lord, who daily loads us with benefits" (Psalm 68:19, NKJV). For there is no room

to load up on good things if our plates are too full of undesirable things.

- Our emotional and mental wellness is important to God. "Dear friend, I pray that you may enjoy good health and that all may go well with you, even as your soul is getting along well" (3 John 1:2, NIV). Our "soul" (mind, will, emotions) was created to get along well with God so things may go well for us. Through Christ, we have peace and access to God 24/7 and can live every moment getting along with God. Unhealthy emotions and thoughts put us in conflict with God's spirit (or God), and it stops and hinders the work of God in our lives.

- Our spirit (represents our spiritual life), soul (represents our emotional and mental health), and body (represents our physical health) are all interconnected, and a dysfunction in one area can impact other areas. God is so gracious that He wants us to come to Him to keep our lives firing on all cylinders. I do believe we need to be emotionally strong, mentally strong, spiritually strong, and physically strong to fulfill our God-designed purposes and destiny.

- We cannot go any further than our thoughts. "For as he thinks in his heart, so is he" (Proverbs 23:7a, NKJV). Our thoughts can trap us. David understood he had a big destiny to fulfill (after all, he was anointed to be the king of Israel) but to get there, he needed to address his heart issues with the Lord and bring his soul in alignment with God. I absolutely love verse 5 of Psalm 142: where David brings his mind and emotions under the truth of God (making his soul to get along with God) and declares: "You are my place of refuge. You are all I really want in life." What David would be saying is something like this, "What people or circumstances have done to me hurts deeply, but they are not my helper, my refuge, my safety, my justice, my protection, or my success. Neither can they stop the plans of God over my life. It would be nice if they were on my side, but it doesn't matter because I have you (God) on my side, you got me, you are for me, you are with me, never to leave me or forsake me. God, I am at peace with who you are for me. I can let go of the people who weren't there for me, treated me unjustly because I have you, my God. Your love and care for me far outweigh anything bad that was done to me."

- David teaches us that we will face difficult people and circumstances on the path to fulfilling our destiny. "These things I have spoken to you, that in Me you may have peace. In the world you will have tribulation; but be of good cheer, I have overcome the world" (John 16:33, NKJV). Expect curveballs and unexpected twists and turns—how you deal with these will determine the next steps. You can get stuck and be put on pause until you learn to make your soul (mind, will, emotions) get along with God. I wish I knew this truth a long time ago!

- What you experience is not unique—the enemy makes you feel like you are an oddball, something is wrong with you, and problems only happen to you. Not so! 1 Peter 5:9 (NLT): "Stand firm against him and be strong in your faith. Remember that your family of believers all over the world is going through the same kind of suffering you are."

Battles may vary, but God gives us an oversupply of custom-made grace for every challenge, and He already has the victory.

- We all have only a limited amount of mental and emotional energy—we get to decide how we are going to spend it. When you expend energy on unimportant things, you won't have energy for what is truly important.
- We were created to be a well-oiled machine with our thoughts in sync with God's thoughts. When thoughts are conflicted, it stops the flow of God's spirit in our lives. We will be unable to think right, speak right and therefore act right. We become too focused on our problems that we are unable to come up with solutions—our creative mind becomes jarred. I know all too well!
- To get help, you need to get very good at asking and receiving help. Jesus will knock on our door; it's up to us to open the door and respond to Him (Revelation 3:20). King David knew he didn't have the strength in himself—He needed God, and He came to his rescue every time. Jesus gives us an extraordinary invitation to live in rest (refreshment, cessation from our own labor) because He has worked everything out for your life: "Come to Me, all you who labor and are heavy laden, and I will give you rest. Take My yoke upon you and learn from Me, for I am gentle and lowly in heart, and you will find rest for your souls. For My yoke is easy and My burden is light" (Matthew 11:28-30, NKJV).
- We trust in a God who is highly qualified and willing to fight our every battle (2 Chronicles 20:15;

1 Samuel 17:47). Christ in us will triumph every challenge, so He will receive all the praise for the outcome. Our primary job is to release control, trust and come in agreement with Him. Did you know what distresses you (how big or small) distresses God? "In all their distress He too was distressed, and the angel of His presence saved them. In His love and mercy, He redeemed them; He lifted them up and carried them all the days of old" (Isaiah 63:9, NIV).

- It is a lot easier to take care of emotional wounds as they happen and not let them take root and develop life on their own. I believe it's why God instructed us in Ephesians 4:26 (NLT), "And don't sin by letting anger control you. Don't let the sun go down while you are still angry." The next verse instructs to give no place to the devil. If at the end of the day, you still feel frustrated, upset, fearful, mad, and bend out of shape of whatever happened that day, including how you spoke or acted, it's a good sign you need to get alone with God and bring it to Him and pour your heart before Him. We need to release and let go of whatever we allowed to "control" us and now got contaminated with our recreated beautiful spirit. It is also a sign that the old nature is reigning, so it is a good opportunity to reckon yourself dead to that old nature. Always rest in the truth that you are God's beloved child; you are in right standing with God and are eternally safe with Jesus, so the enemy does not make you feel less than who you are. Because you are in Christ, His blood always speaks for you, and His righteousness covers you.

- We are designed to be controlled and ruled by the Holy Spirit, not by our opinions or by others. "But I say, walk by the Spirit, and you will not gratify the desires of the flesh" (Galatians 5:16, ESV). To walk by the Spirit, we need to grow in the spirit.

- Ultimately, the highest goal is living in "360-degree Jesus" (that I referred to earlier) in the God cycle—depending on what God has already provided for you through Christ—an abundance of God's goodness, grace, mercy, peace, righteousness, promises, faithfulness, and His great love and coming to the point of inner growth where what God is constantly supplying to you through Christ is far above any pain, hurts, and challenges of this life.

JESUS: UP AND CLOSE

The next several chapters will look more closely at Jesus because, without Him, you are nothing, you can do nothing and will never overcome. But, in Him, you have everything!

I was drawn to the gospels to see Jesus in action. Jesus makes a statement that anyone who has seen me has seen the Father (John 14:9). Jesus says, "My Father has entrusted everything to me. No one truly knows the Son except the Father, and no one truly knows the Father except the Son and those to whom the Son chooses to reveal Him" (Matthew 11:27, NLT). Jesus came to reveal to us the Father. I had an invitation to know the Father, and I was drawn to look more closely at Jesus to get a glimpse of my heavenly Father!

It's important to lay hold of Jesus, the author of our salvation and the finisher of our faith. Jesus came for the lost sheep, for the unhealthy and the sick. He did not come to call those who think they are righteous but those who know they are sinners (Matthew 9:12; Luke 5:32). Jesus came to save the sinners (criminals, outlaws, offenders, malefactors, reprobates) and ate with the scum (1 Timothy 1:15; Matthew 9:10). Everyone was a sinner, but not everyone had the same awareness of their sin.

If you didn't think you were dead, a captive, blind, oppressed, brokenhearted and poor without Christ, you missed Him (reference to Luke 4:18). If you didn't see yourself as an uncharged dead cell phone with no access to a power cord or outlet, you would miss Him. It bothered the Pharisees that they questioned why a holy consecrated Rabbi would be so comfortable around outlaws, offenders, and lepers—it made no sense. Surely, He couldn't be the Messiah. To top it all, what blasphemy that Jesus would tell people that their sins are forgiven? The encounters with Jesus were like no other ever seen before.

- What prompted such a radical turnaround for Mary Magdalene (who had seven demons), the Samaritan woman (who had five husbands), and Zacchaeus (a seasoned extortioner)?
- Why did the Samaritan woman not cover up or justify her bad history or feel any shame when Jesus confronted her?
- Why did the woman caught in adultery not feel ashamed or condemned in the presence of most Holy God?
- Why was Jesus so comfortable with the outlaws and lawbreakers?
- How could He eat with sinners? Didn't Psalm 1 tell us not to walk or stand or sit in the company of mockers/sinners? Weren't these sinners and wicked people like worthless chaff that were going to be scattered by the wind?
- How did these sinners have a place at the same table as the King of glory? Why didn't they get consumed in the holiness of Jesus? After all, no one can see the face of God and live, and even Moses had to settle to see the backside of God (Exodus 33:20, 23).
- How did Jesus tolerate such rogue disciples? Why would He even pick them, knowing they were

going to be a piece of work, would deny and bring Him pain and couldn't be with Him even at His lowest point at the garden of Gethsemane?

- How could Jesus violate the law in Leviticus 13:45-46, touch the leper and heal him (Matthew 8:3; Luke 5:13; Mark 1:41)? Based on the old testament, "He shall be unclean. All the days he has the sore he shall be unclean. He is unclean, and he shall dwell alone; his dwelling shall be outside the camp" (Leviticus 13:46, NKJV). He touched and healed the worst leper to prove a point. Was it a coincidence that Jesus also suffered outside the camp (outside the gates)? Not at all! God did this so that through Christ, He can bring all the outsiders, isolated and the most marginalized and disqualified ones, to dwell near Him. I was one of those outsiders! Because of Jesus, no one is out of reach, needs to live alone or outside the camp. Jesus broke every barrier to *life*! Jesus carried *all* the possible uncleanness of all the world on the cross, so He would be the only one qualified to reach out, touch the most unclean person and make them clean forever. The healing, purity, and righteousness of Jesus flowed to the leper as his uncleanness, open sores, and disfigurement came on Jesus.

This is the best news ever, the gospel, the great exchange of death to life, and this is our Jesus! Hallelujah! He does what no one else can.

In all these instances, it is the holiness and righteousness of Jesus that drove the result, not the wickedness and uncleanness of man. It didn't matter how blind, how oppressed, how sinful someone was—the perfection of Jesus was more than enough. God so loved the leper, the Samaritan woman, the woman caught in adultery, you and I, that He gave us Jesus, the most beloved *One*, that through Him, God reconciled the world of its sin once and for all time. Sin was like deadly cancer that permeated from Adam, which was finished at the cross. Jesus broke every wall, every separation and tore down the veil, and took every grossness of our sin nature on Him, so our heavenly Father can get all His children back to Him.

Every healing and deliverance that Jesus performed on the earth was God's opportunity to reveal the power, the greatness, the righteousness, and the purity of the superstar of all superstars, Jesus Christ! It wasn't about how big someone's sin or sickness was, which was what the Pharisees constantly focused on, but it was about how big Jesus was. Jesus has conquered our sin nature and what the enemy has accomplished through the bondage of sin.

"For the law was given through Moses, but grace and truth came through Jesus Christ" (John 1:17, NKJV). While the law declared the leper unclean, Jesus comes with heaven's reality of grace and truth and declared him "clean." The Pharisees missed that Jesus came to fulfill the law, so grace and truth which came through Christ can now reign.

With every person and situation, Jesus proved that "Where sin abounded, grace abounded much more" (Romans 5:20b, NKJV). Jesus demonstrated that the grace (undeserved favor and goodwill) that the Father sent through Jesus to this world was infinitely greater than any mistake, failure, or effect of sin for anyone who truly believed in Him.

> Yes, Adam's one sin brings condemnation for everyone, but Christ's one act of righteousness brings a right relationship with God and new life for every-

one. Because one person disobeyed God, many became sinners. But because one other person obeyed God, many will be made righteous. God's law was given so that all people could see how sinful they were. But as people sinned more and more, God's wonderful grace became more abundant. So just as sin ruled over all people and brought them to death, now God's wonderful grace rules instead, giving us right standing with God and resulting in eternal life through Jesus Christ our Lord.

Romans 5:18-21 (NLT)

Meditate on these powerful scriptures. Because of Jesus, sin no longer rules us, leading to death and defeat instead, God's wonderful grace rules leading us to life and victory! Please ask the Holy Spirit to reveal Jesus to you in greater depths—He is the key to walking in victory.

The meaning of Behold = To fix the eyes upon; to see with attention; to observe with care (KJV dictionary definition). See or observe (a thing or person, especially a remarkable or impressive one) (online definition). There is no one more remarkable, impressive, or worthy than Jesus! This is why He will be the only one who will be eternally praised and adored. Behold Him!

BEHOLD (see, observe with care, fix your eyes) the Jesus of your salvation:

- **BEHOLD** what manner of love the Father has bestowed on us, that we should be called children of God! (1 John 3:1a, NKJV).

- **BEHOLD** the lamb of God which taketh away the sin of the world (John 1:36b, KJV).
- And the angel said unto them, Fear not: for, **BEHOLD**, I bring you good tidings of great joy, which shall be to all people (Luke 2:10, KJV). Jesus became our good tidings of great joy!
- **BEHOLD**, I lay in Zion A chief cornerstone, elect, precious, and He who believes on Him will by no means be put to shame (1 Peter 2:6, NKJV). Jesus is our chief cornerstone, elect and precious and His hope never disappoints us (Romans 5:5).
- I am He who lives, and was dead, and **BEHOLD**, I am alive forevermore. Amen. And I have the keys of Hades and of Death (Revelation 1:18, NKJV). Jesus holds the keys of hell and death forever!
- Therefore, if any man be in Christ, he is a new creature: old things are passed away; **BEHOLD**, all things are become new (2 Corinthians 5:17 KJV). Thanks to Jesus, ALL things have become new for us who are in Christ.

Jesus came to proclaim release to the captives, to give sight to the blind, freedom for the oppressed, to bring the good news to the poor, and to declare the year of the Lord's favor (Luke 4:18). This is the gospel—God's free and undeserving grace, unfailing mercy, and unconditional love towards us taking us from death to life, recreating us to what God intended in His original design, and establishing us as His children under a powerful new covenant in His blood.

Jesus is infinite—it doesn't matter how worse of a person you are; Jesus is infinitely greater than you. For those of you who are Math whiz's, infinity divided by one hundred or infinity divided by 1,000,000,000 is still infinity. It is the numerator that drives the result, not the denominator, when the One on the top is the impregnable, Jesus Christ. The inferior/lesser (we) were blessed and transformed by the Superior/greater (Jesus Christ) (Hebrews 7:7). Jesus is infinitely bigger, and the blood of Jesus is the supreme cleanser. If you are in Christ and disqualifying yourself based on your sins, you are indirectly disqualifying Jesus. You have taken Jesus out of the numerator. Your salvation, your life now through eternity, is held together in Jesus—everything falls apart without Him. Because Jesus is the numerator and our head, as we yield to Him, the resurrection and life will flow into every part of our life where there may be death, decay, and destruction. Jesus is that powerful!

We go from being a stunted shrub in a desert to an oak of righteousness in Christ. In our sinful nature, we are cursed as we only know to put our trust in ourselves, in mere humans, and only rely on human strength with hearts that turn away from God. Without connected to Christ, this is our picture, and we are like stunted shrubs in the desert without hope, living in the barren wilderness, in an uninhabited salty land (Jeremiah 17:5-6). It is all about us, reliance on us and others, and we become fruitless, visionless, purposeless, and hopeless.

In Christ, we were recreated to be like trees planted along a riverbank with roots that reach deep into the water. Such trees are not bothered by the heat or worried by long months of drought; their leaves stay green because they are abiding in Christ (Jeremiah 17:7-8). They are full of life, producing continuous fruit regardless of circumstances or harsh elements of this life. To remain in Christ and in the God cycle, we will need to depend on Christ solely: living by faith in "360-degree Jesus," who is in you, with you, for you, above you, underneath you, and surrounding you!

JESUS IN ACTION: THROUGH THE STORY OF WOMEN AT THE WELL

I love this story! Jesus walks about thirty-six miles from Judea to Samaria[1] to meet the woman at the well; that would be about nine to twelve hours of walking. Jesus would leave his disciples, walk all alone for nine to twelve hours in the heat to save a moral pariah and a racial outcast. Jesus arrives at the well about noontime, so my guess is he had to start walking at about three a.m. in the morning, assuming he made the trek in one day. To top it off, Jesus breaks the protocol for a rabbi not to be talking to any woman in public. She is of the wrong race/ethnicity, wrong gender, morally bankrupt woman with a terrible reputation. Everything about her is wrong. I personally don't know anyone who has had five husbands and went through five divorces and now has a live-in boyfriend. This was the background of this woman over 2,000 years ago.

I am surprised she wasn't stoned or killed for her moral issues or didn't kill herself, and she survived to meet Jesus. I picture this woman to be charming and beautiful but a drama queen—most people have trouble finding one person to get

---

[1] https://www.bible-history.com/map_jesus/MAPJESUSNew_Testament_Cities_Distances.htm (estimated distance from Jerusalem, capital city of Judea to Samaria).

married, she seems to have no problem finding six men! God had a beautiful design for her life with her attractive personality and good looks, but my guess is that it was used and abused in ways that left her in much pain, disappointment, and misery. She no longer believed in marriage and ended up moving in with her current boyfriend. I think Jesus came alone without his disciples to meet with this woman because they weren't ready to understand the depth of the Father's heart for a woman like this. God would have Jesus arrive at the well around the same time as when the Samaritan woman would be coming to draw water that day. They say she came to the well in the afternoon to avoid sneers and ridicule from other women, who would come during the morning hours before it got too hot to walk.

Surprisingly, she does not feel threatened or offended when Jesus asks about her husbands or about her failed marriage history. She doesn't cover up; in fact, she feels safe in His presence and engages with Jesus in an honest conversation. She is surprised this Jewish Rabbi would ask her for a drink, let alone be interested in talking to her. Jesus did not come to reveal how sinful she was; He came to set this woman free from her vicious cycle of sin. I think Jesus tells her about her marriage history not only to reveal Himself but also to let her know that He knows every detail of her past mistakes and failures, but that doesn't stop the King of the universe from pursuing her, that He is the God that leaves the ninety-nine righteous ones in search of her and has come to this well to reset her life. God is in the business of saving, not condemning the world (John 3:17). Are we in our Father's business?

This woman would become the first evangelist! I love God's picking—He is so non—traditional, so counterintuitive to human thinking, so glorious in grace. We see a completely different woman after her encounter with Jesus—she becomes bold and confident, filled with dignity; she faces and runs to the people she has avoided all these years. She is no longer insecure or filled with shame. In the presence of Jesus, she receives love for the people who have hurt her, talked behind her back, and treated her badly; now, she doesn't want them to miss the opportunity to meet this amazing Messiah. What a savior! She leaves an important part of her physical survival (her water pot) and runs to rally up her village to meet the Living Water who can quench the real dehydration in people's hearts. She boldly lets the people of the village know of the prophet and Messiah.

God gave her what she didn't have or could ever get on her own. One would expect this woman to have no influence to convince anyone to come and see the Messiah; after all, she is not a believable character, a woman with no voice, no power, a complete failure—no one would care to listen to her, let alone drop what they were doing impromptu to come to meet this so-called Messiah based on her reputation. But the villagers not only come running to meet Jesus, but they also couldn't get enough of Jesus and begged him to stay two more days, and many believed and followed Jesus through an obscure woman. She started the first revival in that village. She made history as the first revivalist too!

She was filled with the warmth of the Messiah's love and was welcomed to the Family of God. She became lit on the inside by the Author of Life as she walked with spring in her steps and was transformed in the presence of Jesus. It was not about the Samaritan woman; it was about who she was designed to be in Christ and the wonderful effects of Christ's *life* that was produced on the inside of her as she went from death to life.

She received the righteousness of God as she believed in Jesus. He became her sin, and she became God's righteousness in exchange (2 Corinthians 5:21). When she lied, cheated on her husband, got angry, said hateful words, walked out of her home, God only saw what Jesus would have said or done and how Jesus would have reacted. God loved this woman as much as He loved Jesus. While others saw her baggage outside of Christ and wrote her off, her heavenly Father saw her in Christ (without the disease of sin, perfect in Christ).

With God's righteousness upon her, God saw her as a great oak of righteousness, a planting of the Lord for the display of His splendor (Isaiah 61:3b). Interestingly, the oak tree is one of the most loved trees in the world, one of the tallest living things in the landscape, and is a symbol of strength, durability, resistance, and knowledge. The oak has been represented in different mythologies and even linked to powerful gods. Because of God's righteousness upon her, she became bold and courageous, for "the righteous are as bold like a lion" (Proverbs 28:1).

While everyone else saw a scandalous woman, who was beyond repair and out of whom nothing good could possibly come out, Jesus saw an honorable woman, who was highly significant and precious to her Father in heaven. While everyone gossiped behind her back, God saw a powerful influencer, evangelist, and revivalist. God is known for His reputation to choose those who are weak and foolish (1 Corinthians 1:27). This is the great gospel that has the power of God to save! It does the same for everyone because it is not about people; it is about Jesus.

Gospel is the power and the wisdom of God to release us from our captivity, to get us out of our prisons, to heal our broken hearts like the Samaritan woman. The gospel of Jesus Christ sets us free to see others in Christ alone and not by our cultural attitudes, biases, or prejudices. Gospel is Jesus taking our ashes and giving us a crown of beauty; it is Jesus taking our mourning and giving us a joyous blessing, taking our despair, and giving us festive praise (Isaiah 61:3a). It is Jesus taking our full package of mess and giving us all of Himself!

The gospel is change in ownership—Jesus came to proclaim the year of the Lord's favor upon people (the year of Jubilee in Leviticus 25). Jesus purchased freedom for all 7.8 billion people living in the world right now, but not everyone has received Christ and accepted His free gift. The year of Jubilee (every fiftieth year) was a reset year—the land would go back to the original owner. I love that through Christ, God did a reset on mankind and restored us to our original owner, God Himself. Those of us who have accepted Christ now belong to our original owner and creator, Papa God!

Because we are placed in Christ, as far as God is concerned, we say, act, and behave like Jesus does when our current behavior could be far from it. Sanctification (or beautification) is bridging or closing the gap between how God sees us in Christ versus our current attitudes and behavior. Something's not right if we cannot overcome our insecurities, fear, pride, addictions, jealousy, and shame sitting in churches for decades at a time. We need to ask if we truly understood the gospel. Have we encountered the person of the gospel, Jesus Christ?

May God open your inner eyes to see yourself, others, and all your problems in Christ. If you are in Christ, your challenges are in Christ too. Imagine Jesus as a gigantic box and see your problem in that box. Cast every problem into the box. If you see anyone or anything without first seeing the box first (Jesus), you will have no hope or faith to stand on. You will fall apart. Faith in Christ is the only thing that will give us legs to stand on. If you don't see Jesus first, you will judge based on your opinions and perspectives or what everyone else is saying. When you see Jesus first, you see the most loving, powerful, and exalted *One* in the whole universe. Through the eyes of faith, see yourself, others, your addictions, health struggles, children, finances, and your future inside of the big box (Jesus). Don't judge by the merit of the one inside—their mess-ups, failures, or faults. Judge by the qualification of Jesus! He did not come for the prim and proper, but for the broken and the messed up. His grace, healing, restoration, power, and redemption are exceedingly more than enough for every problem. He loves to repeat what He did for the Samaritan woman. It was God's work of grace in her. All she did was believe and trust in Jesus. The rest is history!

WHAT CAMP DO YOU LIVE IN?

Having received such a great salvation, I believe we can end up in one of the three camps (the choice is yours). I have borrowed the parable of the prodigal son in Luke 15 to illustrate the three different camps:

- Camp one: like the prodigal son, you returned to the Father's house and decided to stay in the Father's house for good. This became your permanent address. This is the place we are meant to live and flourish.
- Camp two: like the prodigal son, you came into the Father's house, but you never made it your permanent address.
- Camp three: you were a prodigal at one point, who came to the Father's house, but you are living like the elder brother in the prodigal son story—staying in the Father's house, but you have a contract type arrangement with the Father not a covenant relationship with Him.

We will go into greater detail of what these camps look like.

Camp one: like the prodigal son, you returned to the Father's house and decided to stay in the Father's house for good. This became your permanent address.

This should be where we should live and camp: we live like the prodigal son who returns home (Luke 15)—absolutely stunned by the reaction of the Father! Absolutely amazed by how lavish the Father's heart was towards him. The prodigal son was hoping for the best-case scenario—if I could somehow convince my father by crying, pleading, and repeatedly asking forgiveness to be a servant to the Father. Based on his human reasoning, the son knew the Father would be totally justified to say *no* to his request to be even a servant—in fact, it would be fair if the Father told him to get lost and disowned him and allowed him to reap what he sowed.

On the contrary, the son was blown away that the father had been intently looking out and expectedly waiting for his return—with a heart full of love and compassion, plans were already set into motion with a calf that had been fattened, and guest list finalized for the feast. He purchased the highest quality robe, a beautiful ring fitted to his size and ready to go, brand new sandals, and delightfully looking forward to celebrating and reinstating his son.

To his shock, the father did not mention or seem to care that he blew a big portion of his blood and sweat life savings on prostitutes, the tremendous shame he brought to the father and his family by asking for his inheritance prematurely, how much grief he brought to the father by his poor decisions, indulging in wild living, and the sleepless nights the father endured wondering if this son was even alive. The son was shocked that his father did not deal with him as his actions deserved but gave him his unconditional love, unmerited kindness and favor, and unfailing mercy.

What the father did was not justified; in fact, his judgments were totally off balance and off base. Why would anyone in their right mind reward and even celebrate bad behavior? What if this son does not appreciate any of these gestures and continues to live in a destructive cycle and hurt the father again and again? The father gave him what he could never qualify to get, positioned him back to sonship, and spoiled him rotten with redemption and restoration beyond his wildest imagination. The father treated him as though he never sinned, never messed up, never blew it, and never did anything wrong. It's like the father had an "amnesia" of all the terrible things the son did and the destruction and trauma he had caused. Was the father losing his mind in his old age? The kindness of his father was so overwhelming! This seemed too good to be true. Is this really happening, or is my father pulling a string? The son was old enough to realize that there was no free lunch, that what goes around comes around, that you reap what you sow, and fully expected to live in the outcome of his own karma.

Surprisingly, it did not matter to the father what the son did or didn't do. All that mattered to him was the condition of his son's heart: was dead—now alive, was lost—now found. This is what the father was celebrating. The father did not keep a tab of his bad behaviors, ready to put him in timeout, take away his privileges or proceed to teach him a moral lesson. When everyone, including the son, saw himself as undeserving, unqualified, unworthy of such a high honor and celebration, only the father knew the real diagnosis of the problem. The real issue wasn't the son's bad attitudes or horrible behavior; the heart of the matter was his heart itself. The father understood that you could not expect anything good to come out of a dead man. A dead man was going to act dead, behave dead and produce the dead fruits (aka, works of the flesh). Therefore, it did not surprise the father to see the fruit of "death" displayed in his son's sexual immorality, impurity, lustful pleasures, idolatry, hostility, quarreling, jealousy, outbursts of anger, selfish ambition, dissension, division, envy, drunkenness, wild parties (Galatians 5:19-21).

The father knew about the "dead" son's condition that others did not fully grasp, for he was like a storm-tossed, troubled, and afflicted city that is in complete desolation (Isaiah 54:11). The father neither reprimands nor gets angry with his son for his sinful behaviors because that would be barking at the wrong tree. For the very definition of insanity is doing the same thing over and over again and expecting a different result. He knew his son was living on the outside but was dead and decaying on the inside—the father knew he could not expect a different result from his son unless he became alive on the inside.

Such is our remarkable story of redemption and salvation in Christ! If we forget how great of a salvation we have been given, we will fail to make progress in Christ. If we forget that we were once dead, now alive to God, and seated in the heavenly places in Christ Jesus, we will not have fruitful growth in Christ. If we fail to understand that we are not under law, but under God's wonderful grace and truth, which came through Christ, we will not develop on the inside as we should. If we don't realize we already have the robe of righteousness and a ring of acceptance on our finger, Christ will not be formed in us as intended.

Second Peter 1:9 (NLT) says, "But those who fail to develop in this way are shortsighted or blind, forgetting that they have been cleansed from their old sins." This is referring to possessing virtue, knowledge, self-control, perseverance, godliness, brotherly kindness, and love, so we don't become barren or unfruitful. God intends us to grow in these virtues

THE INCREDIBLE GOD CYCLE

and go from strength to strength, glory to glory. If we don't have a proper revelation of where we began, what Jesus has accomplished in us (we are now alive to God in Christ Jesus, holy and blameless before Him in love, forgiven and cleansed, blessed with every spiritual blessing to name a few), we will live shortsighted, even to blindness and fail to mature.

God gave us an unveiled face through Christ (removed our veil and barrier), so we can behold as in a mirror on this side of eternity the glory of the Lord and be transformed into the same image from glory to glory (2 Corinthians 3:18). Lack of growth might be because of how you are seeing yourself (if you are looking at the wrong mirror—someone other than Christ, you can drift back to the old "dead" nature and fall into amnesia). Behold Jesus again! It is important to remind ourselves of the foundational truths of our great salvation and take a hold of Jesus, especially when we detect a lack in spiritual progress.

I have two mirrors in my prayer room as a reminder that I picked up from the dollar store: one with a white frame (representing Christ) and another one with a black frame (representing anything other than Christ). As I look at them, I am reminded to look away from everything else including myself and only look to Jesus, who is my savior, my justifier, my sanctifier, my redeemer, my restorer, my righteousness, my defender, my protector, my perfector, my life, the lamb that was slain for me, my perfect sacrifice, the author and finisher of my faith and the source of all my blessings.

In the earlier verse, it says, "In view of all this, make every effort to respond to God's promises" (2 Peter 1:5a, NLT). We are asked to make every effort since God has given us *everything* that we need for living a godly life through Christ. He has given us great and precious promises, which enable us to share in His divine nature and escape the world's corruption caused by human desires (2 Peter 1:3-4). God's precious promises are not only for supplying our every need and to inherit every blessing He has for us, but also for helping us to grow in Christ and share in His divine nature.

Our fight of faith is to live and thrive in our Father's house: all hell will fight to get you out of the Father's house. It is easy to get distracted by the pain of other fights (whether it is health, marriage, finances, children, ministry), but I believe the ultimate goal of the enemy is to distract you, so you will not permanently live in your Father's house. This is living in the God cycle where your life will be the most fulfilled and impactful as you become a major threat to darkness.

We flourish in our Father's house the same way we started our new life—by faith depending on God's free and undeserving grace. You cannot earn your way into your Father's house. It is your privilege and inheritance to live in your Father's house by:

- Amazed by a Father who would love, honor, and celebrate us when we deserved hell.
- Overwhelmed by the extravagant Father who made us alive in Christ and made us His glorious and rich inheritance.
- Enjoying your Father's presence and trusting in Him fully.
- Mediating and having a revelation of the word of God.
- Confident in a God who began a good work in you.
- Understanding that it is not your merit that got you into the Father's house, and it won't be your efforts and striving that keeps you there.

- It is all about Jesus in the Father's house—it is a house where Christ is the head, and you trust, boast, exalt, put your confidence fully and completely in Christ to stay and remain.
- An ongoing desire and hunger to know Christ and to take a hold of Him.
- Knowing everything you need is already prepared and provided for.
- Celebrating and being thankful for the vastness of the Father's heart towards you.
- Living seated in the heavenly places in Christ Jesus.
- Living under the showers of His unconditional love, unmerited grace, precious promises, and goodness towards you—every day, every moment.

I struggled for many years to fully take a hold of what it means to live in camp one. I heard the Lord whisper to me once, "Stay in My house. This is your permanent residence now. Don't go back to the old rundown house where the power, water supply, and internet have been cut, and nothing works."

When I go astray, I can sense the nudge of the Holy Spirit reminding me to come back to the Father's house. Thankfully, I can also discern when I am out of my Father's house and out of sync with Him. My emotions get out of place—I can sense a lack of peace, comfort, assurance, and confidence in my Father, and fear, unrest, insecurities, self-ishness, and anxiety start to kick in. I don't ever want to go back to the old house by staying in my old thinking patterns.

As long as we live in this world, we will continue to stumble, but there should be a progressive move towards living permanently in our Father's house. We grow in Christ and become more like Him living in the Father's house. When we were born again, we were placed into our Father's new house: seated in the heavenly places in Jesus Christ (Ephesians 2:6). Our address went from hell (dead old nature) to heavenly places next to Christ (new alive God nature).

However, if our old nature that is dead continues to rule over us, essentially, we continue to live in an old rundown house that is considered "uninhabitable" and "unlivable" for a child of God. It's like living in a house with a condemned structure that is ready to be demolished. God is not in the business of renovating our old nature /old house since there is nothing good in it; He paid a premium to get us into His new house. Because a lot of us haven't grown in the knowledge of God, we fail to make a successful transition to our new house and continue to live in our beaten-down house exposed to all the elements of life and unnecessary demonic attacks. We will not be able to fulfill the plans of God over our lives living in an old rundown house.

Check out these powerful scriptures that remind us of our unshakeable covenant with God in Christ and what lengths God went to make sure all our sins were blotted, put out of sight, and once and for all cleared our record, so nothing separates us from His love again. We can securely dwell in our Father's house all the days of our life where goodness and mercy follow us (Psalm 23:6). Otherwise, God would have to kick us out of His house most of the time, since we are still living in our earthly bodies, a "work in progress," learning to live from our new nature and being transformed until we see Jesus face to face. God knew the only way we can grow and consistently live in righteousness, holiness, and reverence before Him is by living next to Him in His house. Our new recreated nature can only flourish in His presence.

David also spoke of this when he described the happiness of those who are declared righteous without working for it: "Oh, what joy for those whose disobedience is forgiven, whose sins are put out of sight. Yes, what joy for those whose record the LORD has cleared of sin.

> Romans 4:6-8 (NLT)

I—yes, I alone—will blot out your sins for my own sake and will never think of them again.

> Isaiah 43:25 (NLT)

Just as I swore in the time of Noah that I would never again let a flood cover the earth, so now I swear that I will never again be angry and punish you. For the mountains may move and the hills disappear, but even then, my faithful love for you will remain. My covenant of blessing will never be broken," says the LORD, who has mercy on you. "O storm-battered city, troubled and desolate! I will rebuild you with precious jewels and make your foundations from lapis lazuli. I will make your towers of sparkling rubies, your gates of shining gems, and your walls of precious stones.

> Isaiah 54:9-12 (NLT)

I will greatly rejoice in the LORD; my soul shall exult in my God, for he has

clothed me with the garments of salvation; he has covered me with the robe
of righteousness, as a bridegroom decks
himself like a priest with a beautiful
headdress, and as a bride adorns herself
with her jewels.

Isaiah 61:10 (ESV)

The Lord is merciful and gracious, slow
to anger, and abounding in mercy. He
will not always strive with us, nor will He
keep His anger forever. He has not dealt
with us according to our sins, nor punished us according to our iniquities. For
as the heavens are high above the earth,
so great is His mercy toward those who
fear Him; as far as the east is from the
west, so far has He removed our trans-
gressions from us.

Psalm 103:8-12 (NKJV)

So now Jesus and the ones He makes holy
have the same Father. That is why Jesus
is not ashamed to call them His brothers
and sisters.

Hebrews 2:11 (NLT)

Jesus is our perfect "elder brother" who is not ashamed
of us, His siblings, even though our behaviors are far from
perfect and we are still being sanctified.

In our ignorance, lack of knowledge, and lack of spiritual growth, we can end up living in camp two.

Camp two: like the prodigal son, you came into the Father's house, but you never made it your permanent address.

I believe this is a broad category: it ranges from people who came into the Father's house with great joy but keep walking away from the Father's house like a dog returning to its vomit or a washed pig returning to the mud (2 Peter 2:22).

This category also includes folks who visit the Father's house on Sundays during worship service but come Tuesday, they are already out of the Father's house until next Sunday morning or next time they connect with God.

You come to the Father's house when you have a problem or when life throws a curveball, but as soon as the problem goes away, you are out of the Father's house.

This also includes sincere believers who unknowingly live in this camp and think this is what life in Christ looks like-pitiful, painful, powerless life with very little joy or peace until we go to heaven. The difference is having a permanent home where you live versus owning a vacation home that you visit occasionally. In this category, the Father's house has become like a vacation home—a home away from home, one that you like to go to visit, relax, have a good time, but you don't live there. It's not your dwelling place; it's not your hiding place, it's not your permanent residence.

This group also involves believers who are tossed between two kingdoms, straddling between light and darkness, getting choked by the cares of this world, the lure of wealth, and the lust for other things. You like the idea of a God as a vacation home that you can choose when to go and when not to go. It's on your terms. It will appear to be working short-term but will be miserable in the long haul.

ARE YOU LIVING UNDER A CONTRACT OR COVENANT?

Camp three: You were a prodigal at one point, who came to the Father's house, but you are living like the elder brother in the prodigal son story (Luke 15)—staying in the Father's house, but you have a contract type arrangement with the Father not a close covenant relationship with Him.

I think this is the most problematic camp you can live in because you have no conscience awareness of the "real" condition of the heart, so it is not easily diagnosed, and therefore, more difficult to cure. You look like the church folk, act like church folk, learned to behave like the church folk, but your heart is dull, and your eyes are blinded. As with camp two, there are varying degrees of what I call an "Elder Brother Syndrome" that we can sincerely live under without knowing. I think the church folks who haven't committed major sins in their lives, cradled into Christianity, with performance-driven tendencies are prone to living like the elder brother; they entered a contract type arrangement with the Father instead of a close relationship with God that is built on trust and love.

I can relate to this group because I had a whole slew of these self-righteous attitudes and hypocrisies. I had no problem seeing the speck in another's eye but was blind to the log in my own eyes. I am forever grateful to God for opening my eyes to His truth! It is amazingly liberating that you never want to live even a minute like an elder brother. This group is prone to deceptions, envy, and jealousy and unable to live a truly transformed life and come into spiritual maturity.

Before we get to the Elder Brother syndrome, let's look more closely at the two brothers in the prodigal son story.

Common themes between the elder and younger brother in the prodigal son story:

- Both were natural brothers (of the same blood) and had a perfect, loving, and a well to do father.
- Both were raised in the same wonderful household. Both ate from the same scrumptious table.
- Both were equally loved and deeply cared for by the father.
- Both brothers received equal inheritance of their father's estate.
- Everything the father had was equally theirs.
- Their lives were better than any fairy tale.
- But both brothers are lost, and only one ends up realizing it.

Differences in life trajectory between the younger and elder brother:

Younger brother	Elder brother
Younger brother is gripped with fear of missing out (FOMO)—he is convinced there is something out there better than what he is currently experiencing at his father's house. So, he asks the	Elder brother has enough sense in him to stay within the comforts and security of his father's house where he is safe and taken care of, but in his heart, he is disengaged and separated from the father. He

THE INCREDIBLE GOD CYCLE

father for his inheritance money prematurely and ventures to a far-off land so he can stay as far away from his father, as possible. The father does not stop him and honors his choice. He separates from the father geographically, mentally, and emotionally with zero connection with the father (no calls, no text messages, no Instagram or Snapchat updates from the son).	is physically near but emotionally distant from the father. He has a "professional" relationship with the father, not a father-son relationship, as the father longed to have.
Money, sex, and entertainment become his god.	Self-righteousness and dutiful performance become his god.
Binges on reckless living. Let's be real—sin is pleasurable, so he is enjoying his newfound freedom, lifestyle, friends, and women that money can attract and buy. He is out of the house and happy as he can be until…	While he doesn't indulge in outward sinful living or wasteful spending, but he is not enjoying his life inside the house either. He is neither here nor there. He is in the house but not a partaker of the father's house.
He realizes the poison of sin and ends up losing everything; he is abandoned, rejected, humiliated, and dying of hunger. He is bankrupt inside and out.	He is polished, alive, rich, and well on the outside and still has all his share of the inheritance estate money but is bankrupt on the inside.
Hitting rock bottom becomes his wake-up call; he comes to his senses and understands why he ended up in this dark place and what to do next. He decides to go back to the father's house, hoping to be received as an employee/servant of the father.	He does not come to his senses or correctly diagnose his problem. Even though he is a son, he has always behaved like an employee/slave of the father.

Differences in what I think transpires between the younger and elder brother in their response to the father:

Younger brother	Elder brother
The younger brother is honest and transparent with his father—I was wrong, and I wronged you. He lives as a grateful recipient of the extravagant kindness and love of the father, who loved the unlovable, made the ineligible eligible, lavishly gave to the undeserving, and promoted the humble. He is in awe of the father who treated him as though he had a perfect track record, who did not ever mention or remind him of his past. He finally understood that in his "lost and dead" state, he will always have a failing record, but that is the past, and now, he is forever "found and alive" with a perfect record. This wasn't about being good or bad but transitioning from death to life. The father gave him a robe, ring, shoes, and a grand celebration party. He brought nothing to the father except tremendous pain and came back empty, wasted, naked, wretched, and bankrupt. Now, everything he owned, including the intangibles on the inside of him (love, joy, peace, sense of belonging, sonship, ability to dream again) came from the father. He had nothing to boast,	The older brother became infuriated and refused to enter the party hall to celebrate the younger's brother's return. I believe the father already knew the inevitable—I think it's the reason why no one was sent right away to inform the elder brother of the good news that his brother had safely come home so he can come home and join the celebration. He ends up discovering on his own as he comes back from the field. The elder brother toots his own resume to the father and says: • Look at me! Look at my stellar track record of faithfulness to you. • Look at my perfect record of obedience to you. • See what a hardworking son I have been to you. • Look what a wonderful son I have been to you, and then goes on to point to his younger brother to make himself look even better and exclaims, "Look, I haven't been like him—a loser, unfaithful, low life, morally bankrupt, who wasted your

THE INCREDIBLE GOD CYCLE

nothing he could take credit for. He understood that all these unearned blessings were because of the father's goodness, not his.

He understood all the false gods (money, power, sex, entertainment) could not come close to what he is experiencing in the father's house. They felt good in the short term, but in the long term left him dehydrated and gasping for air. His eyes were open to see how blessed he is to have a father like his.

He realized he was celebrated and given so much because of the father's great love toward him. He began to see just how good his father is, how faithful he is, how gracious he is towards him. He understood the father was in the business of saving the lost and the dead just like him.

Overtime, as he stayed close to the father, he becomes content and satisfied in his father's house, trusting in the father's radical love, mercy, and compassion towards him. He knows this father will never fail him or abandon him, unlike what people did to him during his reckless living days. His old company cheered him on, befriended him when he had money but turned against him and used, abused, and abandoned him when they found he was no longer of any use to them.

wealth and brought shame to your name."

In his fury, he goes on…

- Where is my party for my faithfulness?
- Where is my celebration for all my hard work?
- Why do you give so much to someone who deserves to be thrown out of the house?
- How could you give this loser everything and restore him like he didn't do anything to hurt you and our family?
- Why do you reward bad behavior and not punish him or at least be cautious to see if he is real?
- Why are you being so unfair?

His logical humanistic mind is absolutely confused, blinded and he lives offended at the father and his younger brother. He is distraught by the grace and mercy of the father towards his younger brother and becomes more distant from the father. In his humanity and justice, what just happened is simply unfathomable.

The elder brother is blinded to the reality of what it means to be a son of an incredible father and lives in a world that is all about me, myself, and I. He lives a miserable life that is driven by himself, his good works, self-glory, right in his

143

At last, he is free of the misgivings and doubt he had of the father; he lives like a much-loved son. He realizes no eye has seen, no ear has heard, and no mind has imagined what the Father has prepared for him and is beyond human comprehension. His father becomes his hero for life; he longs to be more and more like his father. As he hangs out with the father, he is starting to imitate his father, and it becomes a joy for him to serve the father all the days of his life. He enjoys being at his father's house and enjoys his company. For this was an exceedingly abundant more than what he could have asked or imagined life!

own eyes (self-righteousness), and not driven by the father's heart or goodness.

He is a slave in his heart even though he has a birth certificate to prove he is the elder son with covenant blessings and privileges. But the elder son behaved more like a guest in the father's house instead of behaving like a son because the relationship with the father was broken.

He did not need permission to have a feast/party at any time—all the resources of the father belonged to him, and in his kindness, the father had given the elder son access to everything in the house, and nothing was out of his reach. I love the father's endearing response in Luke 15:31 (NLT) to all his misgivings and accusation, "His father said to him, '*Look, dear son, you have always stayed by me, and everything I have is yours.*'"

In his distorted thinking, the elder brother was blinded to the fact that everything that the father had was his. He expected the elder brother to enjoy everything the father freely provided him. He expected him to boldly come and receive what he needed when he needed.

In contrast, the elder son believed the father owed him and did not cherish him when the father never withheld anything from him and loved him just as much as he loved his younger son. The elder son did not understand that ultimately it wasn't about his brother's party, trinkets, or wasted money, but this was about a father's joy who had an opportunity to restore a lost and dead son back to life. He did not understand that the father was in the business of seeking and saving the lost, leaving the ninety-nine righteous sheep in search of the one lost sheep and sweeping the entire house carefully to find one lost coin. The elder brother completely missed the point and lives on the sidelines, upset and resentful when he should have been in the game! How tragic.

SYMPTOMS OF THE ELDER BROTHER SYNDROME

Elder brother in the prodigal son story (Luke 15) showcases himself (lives from his old dead nature) instead of seeing the father's goodness. Because of this, he is unable to trust the father fully or receive from the father or be about the father's business to celebrate the most important occasion of a dead brother coming back to life.

I believe below are some of the symptoms of the Elder Brother syndrome (sadly, I know too well because I lived in this camp for years and alluded it as part of being human!):

- You don't fully understand the depth of God's grace and kindness and, therefore, unable to live under it. You are bothered by the extravagant grace of God and blessings toward others who didn't work as hard as you did, pray and fast as much as you did, weren't as qualified as you, had a lot more sin in their lives than you did or did not give as much or serve God faithfully as you did.
- You question why you don't get a break from God and all the bad stuff that happens to you.
- You are bothered when God in His grace brings the last to be first and messes up your human logic and

reasoning. For example, the parable of the workers in the vineyard (Matthew 20:1-16) doesn't sit well with you—this is where the kingdom of heaven is compared to a landowner who hires workers for his vineyard; he hired them to start working at either nine a.m., twelve p.m., three p.m. or five p.m. At six p.m., when the owner paid all the workers, the ones that came in at nine a.m. were happy until they saw that the workers who came in at five p.m. were paid the same as they did (same pay for working nine hours versus one hour!). You are infuriated by the owner's generosity, question his fairness and judgment when you agreed to come work for one denarius in the first place. You are the nine a.m. crew!

- You live under human justice, human rules, and human reaping and sowing by your definition, not God's.

- You are more sin (self) focused than God-focused—you live based on what you did and didn't do, and therefore, you see and judge others the same way. You struggle to receive grace from God, which is freely given to you.

- Because you are more inward-focused than God-focused, you keep asking what's wrong with you, wrong with others, and wrong with the world. You struggle to see the good in yourself or in others.

- You are critical and tough on yourself; you beat yourself up, you don't have peace with God, and with yourself, you struggle to like yourself and see your infinite value in Christ and who God created you to be. Unintentionally, you end up superimposing yourself on others too.

- You have difficulty seeing yourself holy, beloved, and dearly loved by God; you are mostly driven by sight, not by faith.
- You focus on the outward appearance, judge, and become critical of others based on your yardstick.
- It's all about you and your works (not Christ's). You judge others by what they do as well and unable to give other's grace because you are unable to receive grace for yourself. For you can only give to others out of what you have received from God.
- You fall into comparison traps with others and become easily offended and hurt (which is nothing but pride).
- You feel entitled and felt out. You don't feel the acceptance of the Father; on the contrary, most times, you feel like the Father doesn't value you as He does others, He doesn't treat you as well others, you harbor feelings of rejection by the Father based on what has happened in your life and feel like you are a stepchild and live out these feelings.
- You have limited thinking and false ceilings—you see constraints and limitations in you and others. You belong to the camp of the "cup half empty" or even the camp of the "cup with nothing in it" instead of the "cup that overflows" (Psalm 23:5).
- You live to protect and secure the limited resources of what you have; therefore, you are unable to become a cheerful giver who is connected to God's unlimited supply for you, and you miss out on God's greatest blessings for your life.
- You tend to be irritated when preachers or pastors talk about giving. Because you are unable to see God as your unlimited source and a good Father

who longs to take care of you, you've taken the burden to provide and protect your family. You eat the bread of anxious toil. Therefore, it is "your" hard-earned money and "your" sweat and blood. You are unable to appreciate that everything you have, comes from God because "you" are doing all the work instead of God's grace, making your work easy and light.

- Your world is too small—you only have developed the capacity to truly love those in your small circle or those who are able to love you back.

- You easily fall into envy and jealously, especially when someone else gets what you really wanted or have been praying for.

- You unintentionally become the "least" in the kingdom of God because, in God's kingdom, the greatest is the servant of *all*. Jesus talks about this repeatedly in the gospels (Matthew 20:26, Matthew 23:11, Mark 9:35, Mark 10:43, Luke 22:26). On the contrary, the greatest in the kingdom already know they are the greatest and are free to be a servant.

- Since your world is centered around "you," you live by people's praises/applauses and become easily crushed by people's criticisms. You live to please people because that's how "you" survive, and therefore, you end up giving people a lot of power and control over you instead of giving that to God. You end up living in fear of what people can do to you, which is a dangerous trap and it limits what God can do. "Fear of man is a dangerous trap, but to trust in God means safety" (Proverbs 29:25, TLB).

- You are unable to receive your worth, value, and applause from God; therefore, you are a prisoner to people's opinions and how they think of you instead of living for the audience of *One* (God).

- You struggle to see the power of the cross for you, the power of the blood of Jesus, and have trouble seeing yourself cleansed and holy before God.

- You keep asking forgiveness from God again and again for the same things because you are not fully sure where you stand with God.

- You don't have a vibrant heart or relationship towards God because your eyes are on you, others, your problems, and not Him.

- You expend so much energy trying to justify yourself, your position, show how good you are to others, how right you are, proving yourself when God has already proven you in Christ. You don't realize you have nothing to prove—you are free from yourself and free from others! You don't see yourself as a superstar in God's kingdom and are so free in Christ that you can serve others as if they did no wrong to you!

- You have a difficult time receiving constructive feedbacks from people because you perceive it as how bad you are and do not see it as an opportunity for growth and an indication that you are living from your old dead nature. But to grow, we need to love both discipline and correction. "If you reject discipline, you only harm yourself; but if you listen to correction, you grow in understanding" (Proverbs 15:32, NLT). "To learn, you must love discipline; it is stupid to hate correction" (Proverbs 12:1, NLT).

- You easily come under doubt and unbelief and unable to receive breakthroughs or answers to prayers. For faith is God's language and the only way to please Him, and faith becomes difficult to operate in you.
- You rather wear a mask and pretend like you have it all together than do what it takes to be free. You miss the whole point of why God saved you and made you His beloved.
- Your life has become a performance-based religious service to God without any real life, real transformation, real fruit, without real evidence of God's power or presence. "Having a form of godliness, but denying the power thereof." (2 Timothy 3:5a, NKJV).
- You don't remember the last time you were overwhelmed by God's presence and goodness in your life.

I think we have too many elder brothers in the global church of Jesus Christ, and is one of the main reasons we are not as impactful and powerful as we should be and why the world only mostly knows what we are against but not what we are for.

I think the camp of the elder brother misses both spectrums: you don't fully understand how wretched of a sinner you were (that you deserved hell) or fully understood how much of a saint you are in Christ and how gracious God has been to you. You do not understand how "cold" you were and how beautifully "hot" God recreated you to be; therefore, you have settled in the middle road life (aka, lukewarm). This is a dangerous place to be. I think the words of the angel to the church in Laodicea in Revelation 3:14-20 point to believers who have an Elder Brother syndrome.

Sidebar: it is interesting to me that the following first-born elder brothers in their families (Esau, Cain, Joseph's older brothers) also fell into a similar pattern with their younger brothers (Jacob, Abel, and Joseph), respectively. I think King Saul also fell into an Elder Brother syndrome with King David.

I sometimes wonder if one of the reasons why Apostle Paul (former Saul) had such a dramatic Damascus road experience in Acts 9 and why God encountered him with a sudden light from the sky with an audible voice, knocked him to the ground, blinded his eyes for three days with no food or drink, was to purge him of the self-righteousness and pride and jumpstart his transformation to becoming a Paul (which means small or humble). After all, he would write two-thirds of the new testament with such wonderful revelation of Jesus. He was a top-notch Pharisee (the ones who demanded the strictest obedience to Jewish law) and was educated by Gamaliel (who would be considered a Nobel prize doctor of Jewish law) and was filled with self-righteousness. He thought he was serving God when he was persecuting Jesus. I think God blinds his eyes for three days, so his inner eye could be open to know the truth of the gospel and of Jesus instead of the law that he held so close to His heart. In Acts 9:18, when Ananias prayed, something like scales fell from Paul's eyes, and he received his sight. My personal belief is that those were scales of self-righteousness that fell off, so he could see Jesus in all His fullness, light, and glory.

Sometimes, God takes things away from us and makes us uncomfortable to purge us out of lies and scales, so we can think like Him and come into God's focus. Born into sin, we became "dupes" of God's original design and intentions.

It's like an original designer item versus a dupe/faux version that looks like the original but is not even close. For example, they sell dupe Louie Vuitton bags for $30 when the original could cost you about $2,500. It looks and has the same feel as the original, but the material and craftsmanship are unmatched. You can pick up a dupe bag from the streets like I did from New Your City versus the original is kept guarded /under security at a fine store. The original has a lifetime warranty, whereas the dupe comes with no warranty—it is superficial, weak in structure, and not built to last very much like the elder brother mindset. We settle for a dupe version of ourselves if we don't sit with Jesus to restore us to our original grand design and live in His righteousness from our new nature. Even though we have been born again, we can live and remain in our dupe version—falling apart, unable to withstand life, patched up here and there, pretending no one sees our real condition. I had no understanding that I was living a dupe version of me! I suggest you take time with the Holy Spirit and ask Him to expose any areas of self-righteousness so you can overcome this dangerous mindset and live in freedom. This is a major trap of the enemy.

We will only be satisfied until we live in our new reality in Christ:

- God-focused instead of self-focused
- God-driven instead of self-driven
- God-awareness instead of self-awareness
- God-dependent instead of self-dependent
- God-validated instead of self-validation
- God-rested instead of struggling and striving
- God-minded instead of human reasoning and human evaluations

You were created to live in your Father's house and flourish under a covenant relationship. You will thrive to the extent of your understanding of Him.

> The righteous shall flourish like a palm tree, He shall grow like a cedar in Lebanon. Those who are planted in the house of the LORD shall flourish in the courts of our God. They shall still bear fruit in old age; They shall be fresh and flourishing, To declare that the Lord is upright; He is my rock, and there is no unrighteousness in Him.
> Psalm 92:12-15 (NKJV)

"Who is this coming up from the wilderness, Leaning upon her beloved" (Song of Solomon 8:5a, NKJV)? I love this picture of the Shulamite woman (representing the bride of Christ) coming up from the wilderness (trials of this life) stronger, confident, dependent, secure, an original masterpiece leaning upon her Beloved, Jesus, and not on her own. You are only as strong as the level of your leaning on Christ.

TRAGEDY OF SELF-RIGHTEOUSNESS

I struggled unknowingly with the Elder Brother syndrome (Luke 15, the parable of the prodigal son) until God started opening my eyes to the vastness of His heart because his father's behavior was so incongruent to human reasoning. You can be part of God's family but be blinded like the elder brother. Father wasn't keeping a tally of the sins or evaluating the impact of his son's sin on the father's life, for he knew the problem wasn't sin—the problem was the son was lost and needed to be saved from his sins.

God's grace (God lavishing on us what we do not deserve) and mercy (God not giving us what we do deserve), as seen in this parable, are anti-human concepts. I believe that's why the Bible teaches us to not lean (depend) on our own understanding or opinions (Proverbs 3:5) and tells us that trusting in your own mind makes you a fool (Proverbs 28:26). You can have multiple degrees behind your name, be an overachiever and be highly successful in the world and in ministry and still be a fool if you trust in your own corrupted mind.

I believe the biggest wall between the father and the elder son was self-righteousness, which drove him to be all about himself, his accolades, and trusting his own opinions. Self-righteousness will also be the reason why many "good" people will end up in hell (separated from God), and many believers get stuck in their walk with God and do not grow into maturity. Since it is both deceiving and blinding, you end up not properly diagnosing what the issue is to get free from it.

This is the same spirit /attitude that the Pharisees and Scribes (religious leadership in Jesus's time) had, and not surprisingly, Jesus's harshest words of judgment were to these religious leaders of his day because it is an anti-Christ and an anti-gospel spirit. Jesus's heart was filled with grace and compassion for the prostitutes, lepers, and adulterers but He shunned and resisted the religious leaders who did everything right on the outside. It was the self-righteous folks who were threatened by the gospel and the grace of our Lord Jesus and ultimately wanted Him dead.

In my self-righteousness, it was difficult for me to comprehend that I had committed the most detestable sin of all and had been unknowingly resisting Jesus, whom I thought I was loving and serving well. Below are some scriptures from Jesus Himself (in "red letter" print) unleashing his extreme displeasure towards the religious and the self-righteous:

- "What sorrow awaits you teachers of religious law and you Pharisees. Hypocrites! For you are so careful to clean the outside of the cup and the dish, but inside you are filthy-full of greed and self-indulgence! You blind Pharisee! First, wash the inside of the cup and the dish, and then the outside will become clean, too. What sorrow awaits you teachers of religious law and you Pharisees. Hypocrites! For you are like whitewashed tombs-beautiful on the outside but filled on the inside with dead people's bones and all sorts of impurity. Outwardly you look like righteous people, but inwardly your hearts are filled with hypocrisy and lawlessness" (Matthew 23:25-28, NLT).

- In the same chapter (Matthew 23), Jesus goes on to calling the pharisee (with self-righteous spirit) as snakes, brood of vipers, whitewashed tombs, hypocrites, blind guides, and sons of hell. These qualifiers are more in line with devil himself because self-righteousness is from the pit of hell and is anti-gospel!

- "And Jesus said to them, 'Truly I say to you that the tax collectors and prostitutes will get into the kingdom of God before you'" (Matthew 21:31b, NASB).

- Matthew 23:4 (NLT) says, "They crush people with unbearable religious demands and never lift a finger to ease the burden."

Jesus is making a point that the Pharisees are teaching and demanding people to live holy and righteous when they aren't practicing or living it themselves. What they are preaching (the law) is holy, but people are being crushed under the weight of all the religious rules and demands they need to follow without offering any help to ease their burden. They are fooling themselves and demanding something that they themselves aren't doing. Why? Because Jesus fulfilled the law that no one else could fulfill and only through Christ who made us alive and gave us a new nature, can we even begin to live a righteous life. The way of righteousness is narrow; there is only one person who is righteous enough to take us through it, and His name is Jesus. Only Jesus is perfectly qualified, big enough, and powerful enough to take us through the narrow gate (Matthew 7:13). Jesus goes on to say:

> Everything they do is for show. On their arms they wear extra wide prayer boxes with Scripture verses inside, and they wear robes with extra-long tassels. And they love to sit at the head table at banquets and in the seats of honor in the synagogues. They love to receive respectful greetings as they walk in the marketplaces, and to be called "Rabbi."
>
> Matthew 23:5-7 (NLT)

The self-righteous religious mindset leaves us vulnerable to loving praises, respect, and honor from people instead of receiving these from God. We tend to do things that maximize positive feedback from people and avoid doing things that would take away our praises, respect, and honor from people.

- "For they loved human praise more than the praise of God" (John 12:43, NLT).

Self-righteous attitude limits us from God's best by living to please people and winning the approval of people. It will drive us to love human praise and giving it more attention and importance than what God thinks of us.

- "Our purpose is to please God, not people. He alone examines the motives of our hearts" (1 Thessalonians 2:4b, NLT).

- "Obviously, I'm not trying to win the approval of people, but of God. If pleasing people were my goal, I would not be Christ's servant" (Galatians 1:10, NLT).

> Don't think you are better than you really are. Be honest in your evaluation of yourselves, measuring yourselves by the faith God has given us. Just as our bodies have many parts and each part has a special function, so it is with Christ's body. We are many parts of one body, and we all belong to each other.
> Romans 12:3b-5 (NLT)

Self-righteous attitude puts so much weight on us that we aren't designed to carry. The more we try, the more we will fall apart in our own righteousness (our own resume). We are unable to be sober-minded, have an honest assessment of our self, understand what our gifting is, operate confidently in our gifts and the measure of faith assigned to us. We end up having a distorted evaluation of ourselves because we are looking at our flawed self without Christ's righteousness, and that exercise becomes too painful, letting us know who we are not. We size up people based on our ranking, not fully able to submit to all other parts of the body of Christ, and unable to receive from others as we should. It hinders us in every way.

> Then Jesus told this story to some who had great confidence in their own righteousness and scorned everyone else: "Two men went to the Temple to pray.

One was a Pharisee, and the other was a
despised tax collector. The Pharisee stood
by himself and prayed this prayer: 'I
thank you, God, that I am not like other
people-cheaters, sinners, adulterers. I'm
certainly not like that tax collector! I fast
twice a week, and I give you a tenth of
my income. But the tax collector stood
at a distance and dared not even lift his
eyes to heaven as he prayed. Instead, he
beat his chest in sorrow, saying, 'O God,
be merciful to me, for I am a sinner.' I
tell you, this sinner, not the Pharisee,
returned home justified before God. For
those who exalt themselves will be humbled, and those who humble themselves
will be exalted.

Luke 18:9-14 (NLT)

True humility is depending on Christ not in yourself.
The Pharisee's prayer is focused on himself (I am this and I am
not this)—noticed how many "I"s are in his prayer. He did
not receive anything from God—in fact, he left with "resistance" from God. Self-righteousness is like a wall between
you and God, and I believe this spirit is closely linked to
pride (which is what got Lucifer kicked out of heaven). "God
opposes the proud but gives grace to the humble" (James 4:6,
NLT). God does not resist the sinner; he saves them, but He
strongly resists the proud and the self-righteous. God is not
resisting the person but resisting the spirit which is from the
father of lies.

Why was God so pleased with the crooked tax collector's response in Luke 18?

- He was open and transparent about his sin.
- He cared more about what God thought of him than what people thought.
- He was not going to pretend like he had it together.
- He wanted to live righteously but knew he did not have what it takes to be able to live right.
- He did not trust in his resume/record, for he knew he did not have any good in him.
- He knew he needed God's help, and if God didn't come through, he was not going to get this right.
- He received all the help from God, left home justified, and was exalted by God. I think the tax collector is the hallmark of humility which is a magnet for God's attention and help every time.

Most of us don't pray like the Pharisee, but we have undercurrents of the same mindset when we trust in our resume (good or bad), our good works; therefore, we struggle to receive God's grace and depend completely on Jesus for *everything*. I am spending a lot of time on this topic because it took me years to detect the self-righteousness and pride that blinded me to the truth and freedom we have in Christ. It is not easy to pick up unless the Holy Spirit shows it to us because it travels well below the surface.

Jesus is our savior, justifier, sanctifier, glorifier, and transformer. We are dead without Christ, and the only true life we will ever experience is by depending on Him. It's not our work, it is His work in us, and He alone can and will receive all the credit and all the glory, honor, and praise. Only Christ in us can overcome our problems. The more Christ dwells in you by faith, the more powerful you become. Simple, ordinary jar of clay but powerful as Jesus continues His glorious work on the earth through you. Self-righteousness will make us feel confident when we do everything right and lose our confidence and beat ourselves up when we fail or struggle. If you have a self-righteous mindset, your breastplate of righteousness will be missing in action and its instant death because the breastplate protects your major organs like heart, lungs, and liver. Only the righteousness of God can withstand against the devil's schemes.

Self-righteousness leaves us cold and dead with little spiritual growth, while Jesus is warm, full of life, and glorious. You can be successful in the world and do lots of ministry with self-righteousness and pride and not discern it without the Holy Spirit's help. You cannot live in the God cycle with a self-righteous mindset.

SO CLOSE BUT MISSED IT

Why did the Pharisees come so close to Jesus but miss Him completely? What did they miss?

- The Pharisees did not understand the deadness and the coldness of their spirit (old dead nature), and their only way to *life* was standing in front of them. They thought they were good people—but what good is good when you are dead?
- While the Pharisees saw worthless, sinful people, God the Father and Jesus saw them as holy, blameless, and dearly loved children of God in Christ. For Jesus (the lamb) had been slain from the foundation of the world, and their old nature was killed off in Christ. Jesus had the power to forgive sins.
- While the world saw uneducated, uncivilized disciples that no one else wanted, Jesus saw pillars of the Church that no hell can withstand, and one day their shadows were going to heal people.
- While the Pharisees correctly quoted the scriptures against Jesus's behavior, they missed that all scriptures ultimately pointed to Jesus (John 5:39). They were hung up on the letter of the law while missing the author of the Book and missed the living water,

the Word in the flesh, the fulfillment of the law, the life-giver Himself.

- Jesus was like a magnet for sinners because He was the living water they craved for. They knew the dehydration of sin. They felt no condemnation in Jesus's presence but felt heavy shame, unworthiness, condemnation, and accusation from the Pharisees (religious crowd).

- The Pharisees were stuck in an imperfect old covenant that was all about them and their performance. They missed that the new covenant was all about the greatness and perfection of Jesus, not how unclean the leper was, how possessed the demoniac was, how crooked Zacchaeus was, how many demons Mary Magdalene had, what race the Samaritan women belonged to, or how unclean the woman with constant bleeding was.

- The Pharisees missed that clean or unclean, qualified, or unqualified, righteous, or unrighteous were no longer defined by the law but defined by Jesus Himself.

- The Pharisees missed that Jesus's holiness, purity, and righteousness infinitely surpassed anyone's offenses and sins. Jesus's perfect sacrifice conquered/ swallowed up every sin and every consequence of sin.

- The Pharisees missed that when these people believed in God who sent Jesus, they already passed from death into life and will never be condemned for their sins (John 5: 24).

- The Pharisees categorized sins and didn't realize they were the worst culprits. In their own righteousness, they shunned the free offer of God's gracious gift of righteousness without having to work for it, free from demands, burdens, and struggles. They did not want to receive Jesus and His free gift of righteousness. While they were religious and knew the scriptures well, they failed to realize that without Jesus, they were ceremonially unclean just like the leper and were draped with filthy rags instead of a beautiful robe of God's righteousness that is given through Christ. Isaiah 64:6 (AMP):

For we all have become like one who is [ceremonially] unclean [like a leper], And all our deeds of righteousness are like filthy rags; We all wither *and* decay like a leaf, And our wickedness [our sin, our injustice, our wrongdoing], like the wind, takes us away [carrying us far from God's favor, toward destruction].

- While Pharisees were managing and controlling sin by keeping the unclean and the sinner away, they missed that Jesus, the final Passover lamb took away every sin.

If you have any mindset of the Pharisee, you will struggle to live consistently in the God cycle. In the God cycle, it is not about you; it's all about Jesus. The only way you remain in it, is by exalting Jesus, by understanding how perfect of a sacrificial lamb He was, by thanking Him, by depending, relying, focusing, and keeping your eyes on Jesus not you. None of us can boast except in Jesus. Jesus is more than enough for our salvation, our eternal life, and everything else that we need in this momentary life.

This is close to my heart because my mom, who was a wonderful woman of God, a prayer warrior, a woman of faith, and my hero, went through some struggles with her salvation in the final months of her life. The enemy tried to rock her foundation in Christ with everything that was happening to her physical condition and tried his best to torment her of who she was in Christ. I watched her helpless state but couldn't be of much help since I wasn't very anchored in Christ at that time. I was at the hospital with her, and I still recall even though it's been over twelve years now, my brother, strengthening her from John 10:28-30 (NIV), "I give them eternal life, and they shall never perish; no one will snatch them out of my hand. My Father, who has given them to me, is greater than all; no one can snatch them out of my Father's hand. I and the Father are one." This scripture worked powerfully to assure her of how precious she is.

Devil will fight very hard to get you to believe you are *not* in Christ based on your own works and own righteousness—this will result in unnecessary striving and struggling and a life of stunted spiritual growth. Devil's job is to make you look at you, your resume, your troubles and away from Jesus. Don't let him.

Our response to God to Jesus and the glorious salvation should be (gleaning also from the example of the despised tax collector and the Pharisee's prayers in Luke 18:9-14 based on what to do and what not to do):

- God, I will never be good enough, qualified enough, worthy enough, or be in right standing with you on my own. But you've made me all this and more because of Jesus.
- I am grateful and honored that I am so celebrated by you because of Jesus.

- I am righteous because of your righteousness, I am forever blessed because of Jesus, and anything good in me is because of your goodness flowing through me.
- I am qualified because you have qualified the unqualified.
- You have purposely chosen the weak, the foolish, the powerless, the nobody's of this world to confound the wisdom of this present world, and you've recreated me to be strong, wise, powerful, brave, and confident as Jesus is because I am united with Christ.
- I look away from myself and my problems and look to you, my God. You are truly my Father, my deliverer, my refuge, and my helper.
- I count on you, look to you, rely on you, put my weight on you, and place my confidence in you.
- I receive the abundance of your grace (your undeserved favor and kindness towards me) to deal with and overcome my own limitations and failures. I receive from you the abundance of grace, so I have plenty of grace to give away to those who have hurt me, offended me, and to those who don't deserve to get it.
- In your brilliance, I trust you to cause all things, including my mistakes and failures, to work together for my good and your glory. I trust everything will work out well by the time you are done with it. That's how good you are!
- I know as I call upon you, you will absolutely hear and answer me as any good father responds to their child. I trust your character and your timing for my answers.
- As I am waiting on you, I know you are doing your wonderful work in me, so I will be ready

and equipped to do what you want to accomplish through me.

- I discard my own righteousness, for it is like filthy and smelly rags before you and receive and walk by faith in the greatest gift of your righteousness. I am humbled that you would give me such a prized gift.

- I will not strive or struggle to get anything from you; I know that no good thing will you withhold since you did not spare your most beloved prized possession (Jesus) for me.

- I trust and rest in your love for me, in your unlimited power and brilliance to accomplish what I could never do on my own strength.

- I give my control over to you and unload all my cares, hurts, anxieties, worries, uncertainties to you. Help me to understand nothing is within my control to begin with.

- You are the author and source of everything in my life. Without you, I don't exist, and you powerfully hold all things together—my future, my concerns, my victories are all in you.

- I am not able, but through you, I am well able to do what you have called me to do and accomplish what I cannot do in the natural.

- As I yield to you, I know you are transforming my heart, and I trust you to complete the good work you have started in me.

- What would I do without you! Where would I be without you!

I encourage you to declare this over your life on a regular basis until you believe it.

WHAT'S IN A NAME?

In Genesis 32, we see the story of a man who gets a name change from Jacob (deceiver, trickster, to supplant, over-reach, assail or circumvent) to Israel (Prince of God). It is not Jacob who files a petition for a change of name; it is God who initiates and changes his name.

Jacob is the grandson of Abraham (the Father of faith), an heir of God's chosen covenant family, a family through whom all the earth was going to be blessed, a family that God greatly blessed to be blessing (Genesis 12:2-3). Jacob came into the world chosen and marked by God, yet he lived a couple of decades of his life very different from his covenant. I don't believe his mother Rebecca fully grasped what it meant to live as God's chosen people or understood God's promises over her son's life.

She became part of the problem, and instead of believing that what God had promised for Jacob, He would deliver, she convinces Jacob to disguise, lie and cheat his brother, Esau, to get his father's blessing. They did not have to try so hard and go down this route to receive what God had promised. It reminds me of what his grandmother, Sarah, did to birth "Ishmael" (trying to produce a God blessing by human efforts based on human perspective and in human timing) instead of waiting for the "Isaac" (receiving God's blessing by God's efforts in God's timing). It never works.

Generationally, they seem to repeat the same pattern to much pain and trouble. The entire family gets displaced and torn apart. Jacob becomes a runaway, and now you have Esau full of revenge, waiting for an opportunity to kill his brother for cheating him.

In Chapter 32, Jacob finally had it and decided to get out of Laban's house (leave his uncle's house after twenty years of slaving for him). Laban was greedy, abusive, and deceiving and took advantage of Jacob, and looks like Jacob finally met his match. He hears the terrifying news that Esau is on his way to meet Jacob with 400 men (Genesis 32:6); he cannot go back to Laban, and in front of him, there is "death" staring in his face. Jacob is stuck between a rock and a hard place. This is like what his generations would face hundreds of years later—a red sea in front and Pharaoh and his chariots behind. It was in this evening of utter desperation when there was no logical way out that Jacob gets alone with God and has an encounter with Him. Jacob remembers that he is part of a covenant family, and God's promises still stand over him. He reminded himself of what God has done for him, and is honest with his feelings and emotions and stands on God's promises over him (Genesis 32: 9-12). This is a great example for us in our trials of life, even if it was caused by our own mistakes and folly.

God wants to mark this as a destiny-defining moment for Jacob and lets him wrestle from night until dawn. Jacob is desperate and determined to fight, knowing that this is no ordinary person he is wrestling with, hoping to somehow get a divine intervention to face and survive the next twenty-four hours from the wrath of Esau.

I love verses 27 and 28 (NLT), "What is your name?" the man asked. He replied, "Jacob." "Your name will no longer be Jacob," the man told him. "From now on you will be

THE INCREDIBLE GOD CYCLE

called Israel, because you have fought with God and with men and have won."

I believe God was saying something like this to Jacob:

- Jacob—that is not your real name even though that's on your birth certificate and all legal documents, and your parents named you that!
- You've lived a lie all these years. I did not create you to be a deceiver, a liar, or a cheater.
- In my book in heaven, I recorded your name as *Israel*; you were and through eternity will be an *Israel*, my *Prince*.
- I've waited all these years and looked forward to this moment when, at last, I can give you your new name, your inheritance in *Me*, so you will finally believe who *I am* and whose you are.
- You didn't have to cheat your way to get your blessings, my blessings were meant to overtake you and were always upon your head.
- I never disqualified you. In fact, because of my covenant over you, I am not going to be ashamed of calling you "God of Jacob" (God of a former cheater, trickster, and deceiver).
- This isn't about your track record, Jacob, for if that was the case, I would have disqualified you long ago.
- *I am* your covenant-keeping, promise-keeping, faithful God, and I get to have the privilege to establish you as you believe and trust in *Me*.
- This is about my promise and oath to your grandfather, Abraham. I was fighting to give you the covenant name linked with all its promises. This is about my faithfulness and unfailing love over you.

It is about my word, and I will never change my mind about you.

I believe God gave Jacob a physical disability (dislocated hip) to remind him not to trust his flesh, his viewpoint, his devious ways going forward, but to always trust in the God of Jacob. Jacob absolutely deserved to die in Esau's hands for what he did to him, yet God in His mercy does not allow that to happen. In fact, something so supernatural happens as we read in Genesis 33—Esau ran to meet his brother, embraces him, threw his arms around his neck, kissed him, and they wept. In verse Genesis 33:33, Jacob refers to Esau's face like seeing the face of God! The rage, bitterness, and resentment of over two decades disappear in Esau, and God caused a restoration beyond Jacob's wildest imagination. Wonderful things begin to happen when we believe and trust in our God, who made a covenant with us that cannot be annulled or broken and no longer depend on ourselves to qualify for God's blessings. I believe it blesses the heart of our Father to move on behalf of His covenant children even when we don't deserve a thing. God's heart is too big for a logical, analytical human mind to ever grasp!

Jesus fought to give us a new name

Jesus wrestled on the cross to give us our new name; it doesn't matter what others think of you or have called you or you call yourself (Isaiah 62:2). What Jesus achieved for us is a way superior and a better covenant in His blood than what Jacob ever had. You will choose which name you want to live this short life (under your old name or new name), and your decision will produce very different outcomes.

Let's briefly look at what Jesus had to go through to remove our old labels and old names: He was despised, rejected, became a man of sorrows, was pierced for our rebellion, beaten for our wholeness, crushed for our sins, and whipped for our healing. He carried our weaknesses, was oppressed, treated harshly, was unjustly condemned, and was buried like a criminal. Jesus was satisfied after He saw all that was accomplished by His brutal death. Jesus, the righteous servant, made it possible for us to be counted as righteous (Isaiah 53). Since Jesus went through these horrific mental, emotional, and physical sufferings, everything opposite is now true in our new reality. His pain was worth every agony and the mission of God was highly successful for those who have placed their full confidence in Jesus.

Jesus's face was so disfigured that He seemed hardly human, and from His appearance, one would scarcely know He was a man (Isaiah 52:14). I believe God intended Jesus's face and His appearance to be severely disfigured and dehumanized so the Lord's face would always shine upon us, will be toward us, and we can confidently live under His peace—this enables our Father to be gracious towards us when we don't deserve it much like the prodigal son. Through Christ, God removed every "sin" barrier that existed and placed us under the most powerful covenant in history based on Jesus's achievements. We've received the highest blessing anyone has or can ever receive!

Thank God it is not based on our efforts, for if it was, the covenant would have to be updated at least 100 times a day. God responds, reacts, gives, lavishes, blesses, and loves us as He does with Jesus because we are in Him. Our logical mind (part of our old dead nature) will try to come up with conclusions based on circumstantial evidences in our lives—the enemy will also fight you to believe you are not loved, not blessed, and God doesn't care about you that much. But we walk by faith and not by sight. As you grow in Christ, it will progressively become easier to believe and rest in the realities of our new nature. This is where we come easily under the mighty hand of God, and great things happen because we are living in union with Jesus.

Spoiler alert: In this life, we will all go through troubles and trials for growth and development. But I do believe that God's painful discipline is for those who continue to live in their old corrupted nature producing dead sinful works of the flesh. He loves you too much to leave you on an unfruitful and dead-end path. God allows difficult situations that are totally out of our control to force us into a place of surrender and vulnerability so we can be transitioned to our new nature where Jesus truly becomes our head and our boss. Life gets easier, and great things await you in this place! There is no such measures necessary when we live out of our new nature since we live united with Christ and will always yield God fruits. It is so important we get a hold of Jesus and make progress towards living from our new nature. We will cover these in greater depths in later chapters.

It doesn't matter how grim and bad it looks today, because of Jesus and what He has accomplished for you and the new name you have in heaven, I declare that:

- You are a God pleaser, blessed to be blessing, a victorious overcomer, and an extraordinary heir of the covenant of God in Christ Jesus.
- You are chosen, a builder of God's kingdom and people.
- You are effective and efficient, you are whole, and well, you are precious and honored.

- You are a carrier of His presence, a carrier of His glory, a carrier of God's storehouse to a hurting world.
- You are bold, strong, confident, and fearless as Jesus, and you rule over your spirit well.
- You are peaceful, filled with joy, unspeakable full of glory.
- You are a carrier of God's wisdom, insight, and revelation, and you are a problem solver, not a problem maker.
- You are God's spokesperson; you are a joy and a delight to your heavenly Father; you walk in dominion and are an influencer.
- You will fulfill what was recorded in God's book in heaven (Psalm 139:16) and all of God's great plans and purposes over your life.

May you grow in Christ, so you can walk these out through Christ!

You are under God's hesed!

In my struggles to fully trust God, live free from fear and anxieties and stay focused on Him, I heard the Lord saying in my spirit, "You are under my Hesed."

I had heard of the word "Hesed" years ago but had forgotten what it meant. Hesed is a rich Hebrew word with a broad semantic range—stretching from steadfast love, kindness, faithfulness, goodness, loyalty, favor, righteousness, grace, glory, devotion, and mercy. It expresses God's character as part of His covenant with us executed in the blood of

Jesus. God is abounding in love, and it finds its expression in His covenant people. Because of God's covenant over you:

- You are the object of His steadfast love, unfailing mercies, and kindness.
- You are the object of His undeserved grace and favor.
- You are the object of God's loyalty, commitment, and faithfulness.

God's Hesed over you is based on His righteousness that you freely received through Christ. God can be so gracious to us because He sees Jesus first when He sees us.

I like that Psalm 136 repeats the same phrase, "*His love endures forever,*" twenty-six times to remind His covenant children that His Hesed faithful love and mercy is unfailing, can be counted on, and will endure. God wanted these four powerful words to be deeply embedded in their spirit as they faced difficult battles so their trust will be in Him alone.

His Hesed is upon us even when we are not aware of it or don't deserve it. You can rest on His Hesed even when you don't get the answers you hoped to see or breakthroughs in your timing. His Hesed towards us is based on the strength of God's covenant with us—if it was true in the old covenant established through Abraham (an imperfect man), how much stronger is the covenant we have been established through the perfect lamb of God, Jesus Christ!

We are children of an everlasting covenant with God, and His thoughts towards you are always for good, never to harm you, to give you a hope and a future (Jeremiah 29:11). Don't let the negative circumstances change your perception or question His "Hesed" towards you. As the darkness gets darker in this world, God's Hesed love and faithfulness will surely endure over us.

In Psalm 136, it notes that God did mighty miracles, created the expansive heavens, made the earth inhabitable, with heavenly lights (sun, moon, stars), sustaining the food chain for every living thing all because His Hesed endures forever. He redeemed His people out of bondage and slavery, acted on their behalf with a strong hand and powerful arm, parted the red sea, led them safely, destroyed their enemies, faithfully led them through the long years in the wilderness, struck down mighty and powerful kings too big for them, gave them their inheritance, not because they were so good but because of God's faithful, steadfast love over them that could not be annulled! Even God's judgments came out of His perfect love towards them and were for their ultimate protection and good.

I believe every sin of rebellion and unbelief the children of Israel came under was because they failed to recognize who they were and whose they were. They did not fully take a hold of the God of their covenant like Moses, Joshua or Caleb did; they failed to celebrate and depend on the God of their covenant who had already prepared everything they needed. They failed to see how blessed they were to have the Most High God as their God. Because of this, they became discontent, resorted to complaining and murmuring against God and His leaders. This is a somber scripture in Psalm 78:41 (KJV), "Yea, they turned back and tempted God, and limited the Holy One of Israel." They limited what God could have and would have done in their lives.

We are called to celebrate God's goodness, love, and faithfulness over us and to meditate on His glorious works. We don't meditate on how good we are or how bad we are; we don't meditate on "our works"—how loving we are, how much we gave to God or how faithful we are or how we haven't been loving, giving or faithful. This will keep us in our own vicious self-cycle instead of God cycle. Holy Spirit will convict us of our existing gaps only to migrate us over to living from our new nature so we can bear good fruit.

> I pray that your love will overflow more and more and that you will keep on growing in knowledge and understanding. For I want you to understand what really matters, so that you may live pure and blameless lives until the day of Christ's return. May you always be filled with the fruit of your salvation—the righteous character produced in your life by Jesus Christ—for this will bring much glory and praise to God.
>
> Philippians 1:9-11 (NLT)

Apostle Paul is letting us know what really matters and what is going to outlast this life. God's love is the most excellent way, and it will only overflow from us to the measure of our knowledge and understanding of Christ. God expects our lives to be filled with fruits of righteousness and holiness, which can only be produced by Jesus Himself—this is not produced by our hard work or by our good deeds. This comes only by living from our new nature through Christ—only then will our lives bring much glory and praise to God.

CALLED TO AN IMPOSSIBLE LIFE!

Must-Haves versus Nice-to-Haves

For a good portion of my life, I lived with the idea that there are some absolute requirements (must-haves) for the Christian walk; for example, once you are saved, you get baptized, pray, read the Bible, go to church, worship, pay your tithes, support ministries, serve in church, go to missions trips, if possible, give your best effort to be kind and nice as you can be, do good and stay out of trouble.

I compartmentalized what God said into must-haves versus nice-to-haves. By God's grace, I have good genes, a good upbringing, and godly parents, so I didn't struggle with bigger issues that mess up your life in bigger ways, but there were a lot of things I was missing the mark.

All my "optional" (nice-to-haves) lists were things I absolutely couldn't do on my own strength; it required a higher power (i.e., Holy Spirit) outside of me to make these things happen. I knew that sanctification was a lifetime process, but it didn't concern me that I was missing the mark on these decades at a time either. Below is how I would process these scriptures in my mind:

- Love your enemies—the best I could do is forgive them, not live in the past hurts but loving them?

That's impossible and optional. I didn't want anything to do with people who have hurt me, let alone love them. "If you love those who love you, what reward will you get? Do not even tax collectors do the same?" (Matthew 5:46, NLT). "Then Peter came to him and asked, "Lord, how often should I forgive someone who sins against me? Seven times?" "No, not seven times," Jesus replied, "but seventy times seven!" (Matthew 18:22, NLT). I am sure Jesus didn't mean to literally forgive as though we never hurt and keep on loving. Well, no one can forgive seventy times seven. This is not even realistic!

• "Invoke blessings upon and pray for the happiness of those who curse you, implore God's blessing (favor) upon those who abuse you [who revile, reproach, disparage, and high-handedly misuse you]" (Luke 6:28, AMPC). Yikes! I miserably failed this one with a big "F" in RED across the page. This also depended on the level of harassment and abuse, and the best I could do is ask God to forgive and keep my mouth shut from talking bad about them. I couldn't sincerely ask God to bless (extol, hallow) those who hurt me deeply or rejoice when I saw God bless someone I didn't think deserved it. But the Bible has a lot to say about this. "Bless those who persecute you. Don't curse them; pray that God will bless them" (Romans 12:14, NLT). "But I say to you, love your enemies, bless those who curse you, do good to those who hate you, and pray for those who spitefully use you and persecute you" (Matthew 5:44, NKJV). "To sum up, all of you be harmonious, sympathetic, loving, compassionate, and humble; not returning evil for evil or insult for insult, but giving a blessing instead; for you were called for the very purpose that you would inherit a blessing" (1 Peter 3:8, NASB). We are called to bless when insulted or in the face of evil so we can inherit a blessing. We cannot bless on our own strength, and when we bless in the face of insults and evil, we reverse the cycle of evil for evil and open the door for Jesus to walk into our situation.

- "Do not be overcome by evil but overcome evil with good" (Romans 12:21, NKJV). There is a story behind this scripture! I went to a church youth group event with my son Jonathan when he was very young, and they had asked everyone to come forward and take a scripture/promise card. The team said they had prayed that God would direct each card to whoever it needs to go. Everyone was welcome to come to get a scripture card, including parents. So, I went up too, picked up a card, and saw this scripture with Romans 12:21. I was not too happy, for I was hoping for a scripture that was comforting with a beautiful promise, so I put this one back and picked up another card. Immediately, I sensed a prompt in my spirit letting me know that the first card was the one prepared for me, so I went back to the original card. God, in His mercy, knew how much I had to grow this in this area! This scripture with ten little words that I tried to stay away from became a great blessing and a game-changer for me! It was obvious I couldn't do it on my own strength; God was bringing me to the end of myself, so Christ in me could overcome the evil with good.

- "Rejoice *always*! Pray without ceasing. In everything give thanks" (1 Thessalonians 5:16-18a, NKJV). Always? Continually? In everything? No way! This is not even practical.

- "Do not be anxious about anything, but in every situation, by prayer and petition, with thanksgiving, present your requests to God" (Philippians 4:6, NIV). I struggled with fear, worry, and anxiety, and it depended on what was happening, my environment, and the level of stress I was under.

- "Be holy, for I am holy" (1 Peter 1:16, NKJV). Depends on how you define holiness. I had learned to be satisfied with a level of holiness that was comfortable for me.

- "In humility, count others more significant than yourselves" (Philippians 2:3). This depended on who the "others" were.

- James 1:22 (NLT) says, "But don't just listen to God's word. You must do what it says. Otherwise, you are only fooling yourselves." If you've been going to church all your life but doing only what's doable for you, you are deceiving yourselves.

There were many others, but I think you get the point. God is not expecting our behaviors to be perfect by any means, for none of us will be perfected until we step into glory, but there should be progress and evidence of God's glorious grace upon our lives, enabling us to live out the difficult scriptures and a life that is distinctive from those who don't have Christ. We cannot pick and choose the scriptures to the level of our comfort.

Where was the resurrection power, the same power that raised Jesus from the dead living in me, enabling me to do what I cannot? I knew the resurrection power was infinitely greater than any atomic or hydrogen bombs or nuclear power, but I couldn't seem to harness the power to do what I couldn't do in my own strength. I questioned my salvation—was I truly saved? I may have said the "sinner's prayer" over hundred times since this bothered me, and wasn't sure where the disconnect was. If Jesus is the Resurrection and the *life* and He overcame death and the grave and is living in me, where was He? If Jesus overcame everything there is to overcome in this universe, and *all* power and authority now belong to Jesus, and the enemy at best is a headless serpent, why were the sin and my flesh (old sin nature) getting the upper hand? Why was I self-centered and self-absorbed? I was desperate enough to keep coming to Jesus.

I compared myself to other believers and thought that I was doing better than most, which is one of the worst things you can do. I believed there was more than what I was experiencing in the Christian life, but knew I wasn't making much progress and felt like I was in a kindergarten class repeatedly. Same issues, same scenery, same old cycles. Thank God for His brilliant ways to make us desperate for Him to bring us to Him and teach us how to no longer live from our old nature. I always knew the hand of God was over my life; I knew there was a destiny He had designed, for I've seen His faithfulness many times over but knew I had gaps in my understanding of Him, and my prayer began for growth instead of just survival.

I realized my connection with Jesus was not that strong, so I did the best I could in my own ability, but that quickly ran out of steam with bigger challenges. In my struggles, I got intrigued by 1 John 5:3 (NLT), "Loving God means keeping his commandments, and his commandments *are not burdensome.*" Not burdensome? God's commandments are meant to not be difficult or demanding. Why do I find some of these impossible and challenging to "do"? Jesus says His yoke is easy and His burden is light (Matthew 11:30). God makes it easy and light to do His word through Christ.

By contrast, Matthew 23:4 (NIV) is completely opposite to "easy and light"; it says, "They tie up heavy, cumbersome loads and put them on other people's shoulders, but they themselves are not willing to lift a finger to move them." This is talking about Pharisees and Scribes, who demanded people to follow Moses's law when they themselves couldn't do it. This was heavy and cumbersome! This was more of my experience.

Jesus was my answer, the big missing link; although I loved Him, I did not truly know Him, I had not learned to fully trust what He did, receive from Him, depend, abide or stay connected to Him—my struggle with "doing" the word was not trusting in the WORD himself (Jesus) completely. I talked about Jesus, sang about Jesus, preached about Jesus, but did not learn to lean, depend, or abide fully in Jesus and live out of my new nature. I really didn't know the lover of my soul, but that was about to change. As the Holy Spirit started laying a rock-solid foundation in Christ alone, my life started coming alive on the inside (less living from the old dead nature and more from the new nature in Christ).

The Lord had impressed on my heart once that my life was like a coconut (if you haven't seen a whole picture of a coconut, I encourage you to google to see an image). I come from a tropical place, so I am very familiar with coconut, and I love it. I understood what God was trying to communicate—my real life, which was recreated in Christ, is the inside part of the coconut (white "meat"), and it contains the sweet, refreshing water. This is the most prized and useful part of the coconut. This inside part is surrounded by a hard-inner layer (endocarp), which is surrounded by a fibrous husk (mesocarp) and the final outer layer (exocarp). Our "flesh" that we are born with is like the fibrous husk, which is tough and hardened by sin, hurts, cares of this world, and pain of this life. You cannot live out this Christian life with the fibrous husk. Sanctification (or "Beautification") is God cutting through our unregenerate flesh (getting the husk out) to reveal the white meat and the refreshing water that was created to be like Him. Jesus was always so close to me (He never leaves us), but I could sense His presence progressively more and more as God started to remove the fibrous husk. We cannot experience the richness of His presence with our fibrous husk. The presence of God and living from your new nature is worth fighting for!

As God began cutting through the husk, I started relating to what the disciples on the road to Emmaus experienced (Luke 24:13-35)—their hearts were burning within them as Jesus talked with them on the road and opened the scriptures to them. Interestingly, even though their hearts burned as they talked to Him, and they walked miles with Him, their eyes were not open, for they could not recognize who they were talking to until they sat at the table with Jesus and He took the bread, broke it and they shared of the bread. The earthly bread had to be broken in the hands of the Bread of Life (Jesus) before their eyes opened. Sometimes, God breaks us our "flesh" (a painful process) that should no longer be dictating our lives in the trials of life only to open our inner eyes and migrate us to living from the new nature—we are in His strong hands, and the breaking is carefully designed to open our eyes to the reality of Jesus as we sit at His table and dine with Him. Every trial is an opportunity for a greater revelation of Jesus. Don't settle for just a testimony of how God got you through, also get a revelation of Jesus on the inside of you. Jesus in you is the game changer!

I was always puzzled what Apostle Paul saw to make such a strong claim about Jesus, "But more than that, I count everything as loss compared to the priceless privilege and supreme advantage of knowing Christ Jesus my Lord [and of growing more deeply and thoroughly acquainted with Him—a joy unequaled]. For His sake I have lost everything, and I consider it all garbage, so that I may gain Christ" (Philippians 3:8, AMP). But, now, I could at least see why.

It was freeing to sit with Jesus with no agenda—I didn't have to only come to Him to help me with a Sunday school class, to help me with my work, help me with a sermon, or to help me with my problems. I knew this Jesus was infinitely more interested in everything that concerned me that He meant every word when He made an incredible offer to cast every burden to Him. It thrilled Him to perfect everything that concerned me. It thrilled Him to fight every battle on my behalf. I sat to know Him—for the Holy Spirit to unpack a Jesus I barely knew or understood. I was humbled to know that I was a divinely important person for the King of the universe to invest so much of His time and attention to heal me, deliver me, clean me up, restore my soul and help me grow in Him so I can begin to live from the new nature. *I was no longer bored with Jesus!* Hallelujah!

Jesus is the only one who can make our hearts burn with His word so we can "do" His word. It must start in our hearts first before we can do the word. I was able to do the scriptures I could not ever do on my own strength as I learned to lean more and more on Jesus. It simply astonished me just how much Jesus can accomplish in us. It is not worth a single moment living with pain, resentment, anger, or frustration when we have such a wonderful savior and Lord. The life He called us to is simply *impossible* without Christ and in your old nature! Whether to do His commandments, to do the greater works, to be His ambassador, it is all *impossible*. He has called us to an exciting yet impossible life without Him. We are born full of ourselves, and it takes the work of the Holy Spirit to bring us to the end of ourselves, so we can live crucified so that Christ can live in us and through us instead of us living for us.

CHICKEN OR THE EGG: IDENTIFYING GAPS TO GROWING UP IN CHRIST

In the New Testament, you have already committed adultery with a woman in your heart if you look at a woman with lust (Matthew 5:28) and a murderer if you hate another brother or sister (1 John 3:15). The point being we are simply incapable of living or doing the word without Jesus and in our old nature. We cannot live holy without Jesus. In fact, anything that we do apart from faith is sin (Romans 14:23). We are called to live a life of complete faith in Christ (Galatians 2:20). We are all missing the mark when we live in anything that does not manifest *life* and *faith* of Christ. As we grow in Christ, we will automatically sin less and less. The truth (Jesus) will set you free since He is the truth, the way, and the life. So, the focus should be knowing Christ and getting strong in Him—making the switch from the old nature to the new nature.

This is for people who are sick of their sinful ways and want to sincerely live free from sin, addictions, and other struggles (discard their old dead nature) and become more like Jesus. This is not for people who want to manipulate God's grace to stay in your sin (old nature)—if that's you,

you've completely misunderstood the point of God's glorious (wonderful, magnificent, splendid, celebrated, superb) grace. God's grace (unmerited divine favor on us when we don't deserve it) should result in greater transformation of our inner life by migrating us from our old dead nature to living from our new recreated nature. Sin is a curse; why would anyone who is dead to sin want to stay in a cursed condition?

We are too blessed in Christ to remain in a cursed state. It's choosing vomit over fine dining. Sin takes life away; it is withdrawing life from your account without ever depositing or giving anything to you. It is like swiping your credit card when you have no money in your account, it feels good to get something you really want for the moment, but the statements are piling up and will ultimately bankrupt you. It is a dead-end-life with only momentary promises, it keeps you stuck, unhappy, dehydrated, and steals everything from you.

No one in their right mind will want to choose sin (remain in your old nature), especially if you are a born-again child of God. Sin is worse for a believer because, in addition to the cursed life above, there is also added guilt, shame, accusation, and condemnation. So, it is a double-cursed life for a believer. I am going to give you the benefit of the doubt that most of you desire to live righteous lives, have tried, and failed, gave up, or still struggling.

I remember years ago, reading the familiar Psalm 42:1-2, where David says, "As the deer longs for streams of water, so I long for you, O God. I thirst for God, the living God. When can I go and stand before him?" I recall shutting the Bible and telling God:

> "God, what did David have that I don't have? I don't long for you; I don't thirst for you, I don't feel dehydrated for you,

I don't miss you. What did he see in you that I don't see? What is this longing, this level of thirst that he can't wait for the next meeting with you? I can go without spending any time with you for days at a time." David seemed to have a closeness with God that got my attention and provoked me.

This scripture troubled me, and I knew something was truly missing from my experience/ personal history with God and knew this was one of the primary reasons why despite all his mistakes, God called David a man after His own heart, entrusted him with much and chose Jesus to come through his generation.

I started to believe from David's life that there were no mistakes or failures that would ever stop God from pursuing anyone. God wrote our story, recorded every moment in His book before even one moment came to be, and He is infinitely more interested in us than we will ever be for Him. One of my favorite scriptures is David's final (last) words before his death in 2 Samuel 23: 5 (NLT), "Is it not my family God has chosen? Yes, He has made an everlasting covenant with me. His agreement is arranged and guaranteed in every detail. He will ensure my safety and success."

What a person has to say at the end of their life is significant and are pearls of wisdom given they see more clearly looking back plus this is from one of God's generals, King David. Coming to the end of his life with all the victories and defeats, the many ups and downs, David knew:

- He was chosen by God—David did not choose God; God chose him and his family for His eternal purposes. That gave David tremendous humility and confidence in God and His purposes.

- He believed in the everlasting covenant of God that could not be revoked or nullified.
- He knew he was part of a covenant that came with God's own backing and seal. Because it was instituted in heaven by a God who does not change His mind, it was guaranteed in every detail on the earth, and everything fell into its place in its time.
- He understood it was God's job to ensure David's safety and success. David was simply responding to God's heart towards him.

I bet David would have worried less, feared less, relaxed more, slept more, enjoyed more, trusted more, and worshipped God more if he knew what he knew at the end of his life. This is important for us to take a hold of everything God has taken us a hold for. We are a covenant people under a covenant-keeping God.

The other thought-provoking moment for me was while reading the Book of Acts. I was amazed by what God accomplished through broken vessels like Peter, whose shadows healed people and they turned their world upside down. I could relate to Peter out of all the characters in the new testament because I could see myself in his early personality—rough on the edges, dramatic, someone who jumps the gun, simple at heart but passionate. Acts 4:13 (NIV), "When they saw the courage of Peter and John and realized that they were unschooled, ordinary men, they were astonished, and they took note that these men had been with Jesus." Their only distinguishing factor was they hung out with Jesus. I remember having a conversation with God saying, "God, look at this, these disciples turned their world upside down, but I can't seem to turn my own life upside down, let alone turn someone else's life or the world upside down. Something's not right. What is the problem, God?"

I believe what God did in me was answers to those simple but honest questioning that came from the depth of my broken soul. I am so grateful for a God who never gave up on me.

Looking back, I realize that I did not have a true revelation of God's glorious grace for most of my life. I could talk about it but never understood the gravity of it. I even had reservation for the word "grace" since it had a negative connotation of misusing God's kindness. It did not make sense to my analytical, logical mind, but I started noticing it was everywhere in the Bible. As I scratched the surface, I began to be overwhelmed by God's amazing grace, goodness, love, kindness, and mercy.

Our natural man (flesh; old nature) does not need Jesus; in fact, it thrives without Jesus; we can do what we need to do on our own strength. This is how the non-believers operate in, and you can be very productive, successful and achieve great feats, 100 percent on your own without Jesus and live your life on God's universal grace (undeserved favor of God) which makes the sunrise on the evil and the good and sends the rain on both just and unjust (Matthew 5:45b). Our heavenly Father is so good that He is kind and merciful to the ungrateful and the wicked (Luke 6:35b, 36). Even if you don't want God, He does you good by giving you rain from heaven and fruitful seasons, satisfying your hearts with food and gladness (Acts 14:17) that you don't deserve.

It is interesting that we as believers have no problem believing God's universal grace for all people, for we see it all around us how God blesses the ungodly, but we struggle to receive the glorious grace (and a highly debated topic!) that came to us through Jesus Christ. If God can be that gracious to the wicked, can you comprehend how full of grace, mercy, and kindness He is toward you (His children, His family, His bride)? Why is this difficult to understand? Because we can see what universal grace looks like with our natural eyes, but we can only understand and rely on God's glorious grace through our spiritual eyes and by faith, and that requires us to die to this flesh (old nature).

- "For out of His fullness [the superabundance of His grace and truth] we have all received grace upon grace [spiritual blessing upon spiritual blessing, favor upon favor, and gift heaped upon gift]" (John 1:16, AMP).

God's goodness and kindness lead us to repentance (Romans 2:4), for this is what draws us to Him. It is difficult to repent (change your mind and ways) if you don't believe in God's goodness. As I started to get a revelation of God's glorious grace, I became more certain of where I stood with God; I gained more confidence in Him, and started to pray bolder prayers, and as a bonus, no longer worried whether I was righteous enough to make it to heaven.

- "Yes, and the Lord will deliver me from every evil attack and will bring me safely into His heavenly Kingdom. All glory to God forever and ever! Amen" (2 Timothy 4:18, NLT).
- "Now all glory to God, who is able to keep you from falling away and will bring you with great joy into his glorious presence without a single fault" (Jude 1:24, NLT).

God is able and wants to keep us on the God cycle until we get to our eternal home. It is God's job to bring us safely into His kingdom as we trust in Jesus for everything. I started to worry less as I believed God was not only able but was delighted to be involved in every part of my little life. He takes time to count even the hairs of our head (Luke 12:7)!

God even used Colossians chapters 1, 2, and 3 as part of my physical healing from an autoimmune disease that doesn't have a cure. It was a journey of over 2.5 years as God was working in me, opening my inner eyes, transforming my soul, and in the process was able to fully wean off medication with complete divine healing. I started seeing the eternally glorified Jesus yet so loving and humble through the pages of the scripture!

I began to lose track of time spent in His presence. I began to have a greater appetite for God—our old nature has zero hunger for God, but our new nature can only be sustained by Christ and is designed to be hungry for God's word and His presence. My "smallness" of who God was began to slowly change and was drawn by the vastness of His heart.

The answer to our transformation and freedom is Christ. He is our freedom. We should never see our struggles or others without seeing Jesus first. You will lose the battle. Everything about our new nature is held together in Christ. If you start seeing yourself without Christ, you will fall apart—you will judge yourself based on your opinions or other people's opinions instead of God's opinions.

Most battles are won on the inside first before we see the result on the outside. The only way to keep our faith alive on the inside is in and through Christ. Faith is seeing what God sees and believing what God believes.

I have the following on a sticky note that I pray out loud most days, "Jesus help me to live from my new nature today. To see you FIRST not the situation or the problem. Let me see by faith, your unlimited power, your infinite wisdom, your grace, your glory, your presence, your healing, and your abundant resources for everything I face today. You are more than enough."

Make your appointment with God as part of your daily routine, even if you only have 5-10 min. See the glorified Jesus next to you in your mess, in your brokenness with His unlimited power, infinite wisdom, and grace longing to help you and transform you. You matter so much to God. Even in our mess, He never leaves us or forsakes us. He is near to the brokenhearted and longs to save those who are crushed in spirit (Psalm 34:18). I believe God restores us by helping us live from our new recreated nature in Christ, where restoration will automatically happen.

We are transformed (living from our new nature) by sitting, looking, thinking, meditating, and by coming to Jesus—there is a common theme to all these five action verbs—it is Jesus. All of this will result in the renewing of our minds so our inner man can learn to abide in Christ.

- We are changed as we sit in the heavenly places in Christ Jesus (Ephesians 2:6), not in the earthly realm worried, fearful, and full of cares.
- We are changed as we keep our eyes on Jesus (Hebrews 12:2), not on ourselves, others, or our problems.
- We are changed as we think about what is true, and honorable, and right, and pure, and lovely, and admirable. As we think about things that are excellent and worthy of praise (Philippians 4:8). Only Jesus meets all these criteria.

- We are changed as we meditate on the word of God (Psalm 19:7; 110:130).
- We are changed as we continue to come boldly with confidence to the throne room of grace to receive mercy and grace (Hebrews 4:16).

The primary way we are changed is by the Word—it is an extremely powerful weapon in changing our minds when we consistently meditate on the word. God transitions us to our new nature by changing our thoughts. Romans 12:2 (NLT), "Don't copy the behavior and customs of this world, but let God transform you into a new person by changing the way you think. Then you will learn to know God's will for you, which is good and pleasing and perfect."

As we are blessed to be living in an era with easy access to the Word with Bible Apps and so many versions of the Bible—I encourage you to listen and meditate on the word as you exercise, cook, during your breaks, or when driving. The idea is to keep the word front and center of your mind. Let the word do its job.

- "For the word of God is alive and powerful. It is sharper than the sharpest two-edged sword, cutting between soul and spirit, between joint and marrow. It exposes our innermost thoughts and desires" (Hebrews 4:12, NLT).
- "This book of the law shall not depart from your mouth, but you shall meditate on it day and night, so that you may be careful to do according to all that is written in it; for then you will make your way prosperous, and then you will have success" (Joshua 1:8, ESV).

Therefore, since we are surrounded by such a huge crowd of witnesses to the life of faith, let us strip off every weight that slows us down, especially the sin that so easily trips us up. And let us run with endurance the race God has set before us. We do this by keeping our eyes on Jesus, the champion who initiates and perfects our faith. Because of the joy awaiting him, He endured the cross, disregarding its shame. Now He is seated in the place of honor beside God's throne. Think of all the hostility he endured from sinful people; then you won't become weary and give up.

Hebrews 12:1-3 (NLT)

I believe we have many role models to this life of faith (crowd of witnesses) from Hebrews 11 faith heroes, including believers who have gone before us who are cheering us on. Bible gives us the solution to strip off weights (burdens, cares, regrets, frustration, and stress-symptoms of living from the old nature) that slows our pace and sin that is all too easy to stumble on: the antidote is to keep our eyes on Jesus, not on us. We can endure focusing on our wonderful Savior who endured the cross with all its hostility and disregarded the shame for you and me. Since He endured hostility, we can also endure hostility and ignore the shame through Him. We can never do this in our own flesh (old nature). You were His joy and why He endured. His strength received in our new nature enables us to press forward and upward.

- Isaiah 51:1 (NIV): "Listen to me, you who pursue righteousness and who seek the LORD: Look to the rock from which you were cut and to the quarry from which you were hewn."

You have all the characteristics and DNA of Jesus since you were birthed and cut from the Great Rock (Jesus Christ). The only way to pursue God's righteousness and empower our new nature is to look to the Rock (Lord Jesus) from which we were birthed/ recreated and cut from. If we look to ourselves or others, we will fail, give up and not be able to endure tough times with a good attitude.

We are engraved in the palm of His hands (Isaiah 49:16). I like what it says in one of the translations (TLB), "See, I have tattooed your name upon my palm, and ever before me is a picture of Jerusalem's walls in ruins." We cannot undo ourselves from God's palm—we are not that powerful. Whatever is in ruins and not working in our lives ("our walls") is always before God, and He is working on it. He will never fail you.

Fight for your freedom in Christ and don't settle for bondages. Believe that all bondages are from the old nature that is already done away with and illegally operating. God honors our choice and will only work to the extent we want Him to work. Get rid of old news and old nature talk! The Holy Spirit will help us challenge the lies and false comparison metrics that something is wrong with us; our talents and gifts are insignificant, everyone else has it together. Lies! This is not true of your new nature. Embrace the good news and God talk. I do believe that the biggest enemy to our freedom in Christ is not our challenges, it is ourselves—it is our old patterns, old habits, old thinking from our old nature although unfruitful, it is comfortable and predictable, and change to new nature is uncomfortable and challenges us. But, freedom in Christ is far too precious!

To truly abide in Christ, we need to lose this life (representing the old nature) to receive and accept the freedom that Christ has already purchased. We lose our insecurities, our opinions, our logic and reasonings and gain His thoughts and His mind. I am still learning every day. As a bonus, every time we overcome, we lose the grip of the old dead nature and lay hold of our new nature. Jesus is worth your time now and for eternity. Look to Jesus alone!

WHEN YOU FALL

It's not if you fall, it's when you fall especially as you learn to transition from your old to the new nature. It's like learning to skate or bike. We are all going to fall, but it is important to not stay down for long, get up quickly, ask forgiveness immediately, believe God has already forgiven you and get back on the God cycle and move on with your life, looking to Jesus only.

- "For though the righteous fall seven times, they rise again" (Proverbs 24:16a, NIV).
- "But if we confess our sins to Him, He is faithful and just to forgive us our sins and to cleanse us from all wickedness" (1 John 1:9, NLT).

Our human (old) nature drives us to hide from God's presence among the trees of the garden, much like our fore-fathers (Adam and Eve) did when they sinned and heard the Lord walking (Genesis 3:8). But the mercy of God found them hiding and clothed their nakedness. Believe God keeps His word and will absolutely forgive and cleanse us when we come to Him. He loves that you are asking Him. You don't need long, drawn-out prayers to get back with God. It's not the volume of your words or the quality of your prayers, but it's the power and the blood of Jesus that matters. It's looking away from you and on to Jesus to live in the new nature (Jesus-centric). The old nature always looks to us and away from Jesus (self-centric). The cross has already accounted for your mistakes and already done away with your old nature. God knew the mess we were going to be and all the help we will need to transition to our new nature. Remember that God chooses to see you only through one lens, which is Christ—justified, holy, and righteous. He is only working on one nature—the new recreated you.

We are flawless in heaven because of Jesus even though our behaviors are far from it; if it wasn't the case, we would not be able to step into the most holy place or enter the throne room of grace or be seated in the heavenly places (Hebrews 10:19; Hebrews 4:16; Ephesians 2:6). It's important to get back with God ASAP when you make mistakes because there is no safety outside of God for you, and the enemy is waiting to devour, oppress and suppress you and take you backwards in God.

You cannot use human logic or reasoning when you fall—you use spiritual weapons. If you use the former, you will feel unworthy, come under self-pity, and disqualify yourself. The reason you are falling under sin is because of your "flesh" (old nature); therefore, you cannot use the reasoning of the same faulty flesh to overcome. Don't live or feed that part of you. The enemy will accuse you and put thoughts into your mind that you are a hypocrite, you don't belong to God, He has abandoned you, doesn't care about you, you are out of favor with Him because you've failed Him repeatedly. All of them will sound logical but are not *the Truth*.

It is important not to entertain the enemy's condemning voices. The devil is not your savior and did not die to save you. Why do we listen to an enemy who hates us and wants to destroy us instead of Jesus, who is on our side offering us life abundantly? Refuse the enemy's voice. It's the only way you are going to live free and overcome this life. You overcome by coming under the Great Overcomer, Jesus Christ!

- "Therefore, there is now no condemnation [no guilty verdict, no punishment] for those who are in Christ Jesus [who believe in Him as personal Lord and Savior]" (Romans 8:1, AMP).
- "Who then is the one who condemns? No one. Christ Jesus who died—more than that, who was raised to life—is at the right hand of God and is also interceding for us." (Romans 8:34, NIV)
- I assure you and most solemnly say to you, the person who hears My word [the one who heeds My message], and believes and trusts in Him who sent Me, has (possesses now) eternal life [that is, eternal life actually begins—the believer is transformed], and does not come into judgment and condemnation, but has passed [over] from death into life.

  John 5:24, (AMP)

Because of Jesus, you have passed over from death to life!

Stand on the word of God, reject the enemy's accusations, and get back on the God cycle by simple faith in Christ. You carry your heavenly Father's DNA in your new nature which cannot be undone and is eternal. Your only way out of your bad behaviors/attitudes is to come confidently to your Father's house like the prodigal son (in Luke 15) no matter what you've done—see your Father waiting to celebrate you, full of compassion and mercy, hoping this would be the day you would return. You will waste a lot of time in unnecessary battles and stifle your spiritual growth and relationship with

God if you fail to understand this. Again, God is after your new recreated nature and helping you renew your mind, so you start living from that new nature. He is not wasting His time on your "dead" old nature and is not surprised by the behaviors coming out of it.

What label you believe is important—you will live based on the label you believe. You are not a sinner trying to live sin-free, but you are a co-heir with Christ and an heir of God, learning to live from your new nature. Our label in Christ was not based on our performance (thank God!); it is based on Jesus's performance. You can rest and relax in what Jesus has done and stand in His perfection. We are not called to be holy on our own—we are holy as Jesus is holy and will only be holy to the extent we are connected to Christ. Otherwise, even on our best day, with our old nature, we are not even 0.000001 percent perfect compared to the perfection of Jesus. We stay dependent on Jesus to make us what we are not. Any ounce of holiness and Godlikeness that come out of our lives are only a fruit of our trust in Jesus—the more we trust in Jesus, and the more we look to Him, the more we will be transformed. God richly rewards those who diligently seek Him and the resulting transformation it accomplishes.

We start our born-again journey trusting in Jesus fully and need to continually depend on Him hour by hour, day by day, to remain in Christ.

- Are you trusting in Jesus this hour for your salvation? Or are you trusting in yourself?
- Are your mistakes and failures overriding the cross and the resurrection at this moment?

How do you know you are looking to Jesus? Even with your failing grade, you will experience LIFE every time you turn to Jesus. The Holy Spirit who guides us into all truth will remind you that you are already justified, righteous, and holy in your new nature, and nothing will separate you from God's love (not even you) (Romans 8:38-39). You become secure, confident, and stable in what Jesus has done and in how Jesus sees you. In your own righteousness, you will fall apart, but God's righteousness you received through Christ is like a strong, mighty mountain (Psalm 36:6). As you surrender and hand over your failures to Him, you come away with life, joy, and peace. You learn to strip off the old nature and put on the new nature by yielding to Christ. Jesus can only give us *life* and more of it when we come to Him (John 10:10). Even when the Holy Spirit convicts us, and God disciplines us, it only releases *life*. Your job is to keep trusting in the death and resurrection of Jesus and who He recreated you to be.

For Jesus cannot give us shame, condemnation, or guilt—He paid a heavy price to get rid of that junk. He already dealt with everything "Anti-Life" on the cross. He doesn't have anything else to give you. God integrated you into Christ—You are in Christ, and His spirit is living in you. Christ in you is the hope of glory (Colossians 1:27).

The only way God will deny you is if you plainly deny Him, walk away from Him, reject the Holy Spirit, trample Jesus underfoot, treat the blood of Jesus as ordinary, and insult the Spirit of grace (2 Timothy 2:12, Hebrews 10:29). This is rejecting Jesus and the Holy Spirit. It's rejecting the only source of *life* itself. I believe we have to do some drastic things like deny Him and not want anything to do with Him for God to deny us. I used to get carried away with these scriptures and was afraid whether God has rejected me. God remains faithful even when we are unfaithful, for He cannot deny who He is (2 Timothy 2:13). Thank God it is based on

God's faithfulness, not ours. This is not an excuse to remain unchanged in our old nature but at the same time, not allow the enemy's schemes to hinder our spiritual progress because we don't have confidence in the God of our salvation, and we are flip-flopping on where we stand with God.

I think the flip side of that is also true: if you are a believer living in a perpetual cycle of shame, condemnation, and defeat—you need to ask yourself:

- Do I really understand the power of the blood of the covenant by which I became a child of God?
- Do I understand how holy and powerful the blood of Jesus is by which I was cleansed?
- Am I resisting the Holy Spirit—the spirit of grace and mercy?

It's time that we see our heavenly Father for who He is—the cross should be more than enough proof that God will go to extreme lengths and extreme pain to save us and the lost world. It is His desire that no one perish. You must not want to be saved to escape God's measures to get to you.

I love the story of King Balak and Balaam in Numbers 23, where King Balak tries to hire a so-called prophet Balaam (whose heart is not right with God but He is able to hear from God) to curse the people of Israel, and this mission becomes highly unsuccessful. God speaks through Balaam to King Balak in Numbers 23:19-21 (NKJV) and says, "God is not a man, that He should lie, nor a son of man, that He should repent. Has He said, and will He not do? Or has He spoken, and will He not make it good? Behold, I have received a command to bless; He has blessed, and I cannot reverse it. He has not observed iniquity in Jacob, nor has He seen wickedness in Israel. The Lord, his God, is with him, And the shout of a

King is among them." I believe this was a shadow of our new recreated nature in Christ; no one, including you, can undo what God has blessed!

God chose not to see their iniquity or wickedness even though they were far from perfect, so there would be no opportunity to curse a people group that God has blessed. If God was so merciful in the old covenant, how much more powerful is the blood of Jesus in the new covenant!

Check out Hebrews 6:16-20 (NLT) as part of our new covenant with Jesus as our cornerstone:

> Now when people take an oath, they call on someone greater than themselves to hold them to it. And without any question that oath is binding. God also bound Himself with an oath, so that those who received the promise could be perfectly sure that He would never change His mind. So, God has given both His promise and His oath. These two things are unchangeable because it is impossible for God to lie. Therefore, we who have fled to Him for refuge can have great confidence as we hold to the hope that lies before us. This hope is a strong and trustworthy anchor for our souls. It leads us through the curtain into God's inner sanctuary. Jesus has already gone in there for us. He has become our eternal High Priest in the order of Melchizedek.

Hallelujah!

Numbers 21 talks about how the people of Israel who walked under the pillar of cloud and pillar of fire grew impatient and discouraged with the long journey, and this resulted in complaining and speaking against God and Moses. It goes downhill into negative patterns and exaggeration; they complained there was nothing to eat and nothing to drink, and said they hated the horrible manna (Numbers 21:5) that once tasted like honey wafer to them. So, the Lord sent poisonous snakes among the people, and many were bitten and died. Prior to Jesus, sin was like a deadly cancer and had to be cut away. Thanks to our Lord Jesus, God is not sending poisonous snakes into our homes when we get impatient, murmur, and complain because He has taken our sins, cut away our old nature, but it does open door to the enemy to harass us. I love God's simple solution—He asked Moses to make a replica of a poisonous snake and attach it to a pole and asked the bitten people to simply look at it. They were healed and restored by only looking at this bronze replica of the snake—there was no sacrifice, no altars, no sackcloth. John 3:14-15 refers to Jesus (Son of Man) to be lifted just as Moses lifted up the serpent, so whoever believes in Him may have eternal life! God's wisdom is simple yet powerful because there is no one higher than Jesus.

I have always been baffled with how in 2 Peter 2:7-8, Bible declares Lot as a righteous man not once but twice when his behaviors and actions were far from it. If you read Genesis 13 and 19, we don't see much of any evidence of righteousness in Lot—he made the decision to live among the most wicked people in Sodom; he offered his virgin daughters to be raped by the evil men of Sodom, and at the end, his daughters got him drunk and sleep with their father, and it results in incestuous origins of Moabites and Ammonites, who became nightmare enemy nations for Israel. Even from this incestuous generation of Lot, God raises Ruth, a Moabite who trusted in the Lord Yahweh and became the great grandmother of David and part of Jesus's natural bloodline. God's grace and mercy is beyond human understanding or reasoning!

One thing is clear, Lot acknowledged God's grace and kindness for sparing his life, for he knew it certainly wasn't his qualifications that made it happen, but God's graciousness towards him and God grants his request to escape from Sodom to the little city Zoar (Genesis 19:18-21). If this was true in the Old Testament, how much more in the blood of the new covenant with Jesus. In Christ, we have been declared righteous, and every answer to our prayer and every blessing comes because of our right standing with God through Christ.

In the God cycle, we get to live in what Jesus sowed, not what we have sowed or what others have sowed (good or bad) in our lives. You reap and harvest based on what Jesus sowed, so all the glory eternally will belong to Jesus, not us. I believe this is the exceedingly, abundantly more than what you can ask or imagine life (Ephesians 3:20), but it is based on the level of God's mighty power at work in us and how much of Jesus is actually living inside of us by faith (i.e., how much we are living from the new nature).

Great and glorious things only happen because of what Jesus sowed and us coming into alignment with Jesus; it will not be based on our efforts. It comes by seeking His kingdom and His righteousness (this renews our mind and transforms us) not our goodness. This is a life that our efforts simply cannot buy—it is allowing the King of glory to live through us who has graciously made us the temple of the Holy Spirit (1 Corinthians 6:19).

The old testament (Solomon's) temple is thought to have taken a workforce of over 180,000 and would have cost around 3 to 6 billion dollars in today's cost equivalent and was built over a period of seven years. You are infinitely more priceless and treasured temple because of the spirit of Christ who dwells in you—the former was only a shadow of the new covenant saints who would become the true temple. We are simply vessels, but our value and power are driven by the *One* who lives inside of us.

It's time for us to be "Savior" focused instead of "sin" focused, the former will empower you to live from your new nature, but the latter will keep you stuck in your old nature. We can only bring real impact to the world by bringing them to the cleansing power of the blood of Jesus. We have the answer to the sin problem—it is Jesus. People are hurting badly and turning to counterfeit false gods for help, happiness, and comfort. We have a culture filled with people who have been bitten by fiery serpents (as in Numbers 21), and it is not okay we throw stones at them when we have the bronze serpent (Jesus) who can cure the sin problem and bring them from death to life. We have become moderators of sin, managing sin and moral polices of the culture instead of turning the world upside down with Jesus.

People sin because they are dead in their trespasses, are ruled by their sin nature, and under Satan's dominion. Humanity's old Adamic sin nature cannot be legislated or managed. The sin nature needs to be cut away, and the only *One* who can make us a brand-new creation and circumcise our hearts is Jesus. There is no hope, no real change, no transformation, or reformation without Jesus. God gave all of humanity choices, and He honors our freewill. Even in the garden of Eden, God put the tree of the knowledge of good and evil so Adam and Eve could choose. He did not take away the choice even in a perfect garden despite knowing that they would mess up. We will lose the fight against the enemy and lose the opportunity for a great awakening and harvest if we get sidetracked by people's choices and the gravity of people's sin.

We live righteously only because of a righteous nature that was given to us in Christ. We don't live righteous following a set of rules—they tried in that in the old covenant and it was highly unsuccessful. We live righteously because we are living from our new nature that cannot sin. "Whoever has been born of God does not sin, for His seed remains in him; and he cannot sin, because he has been born of God" (1 John 3:9, NKJV).

Jesus did not come to the world to institute new laws against sinful behaviors; if anyone could do it, it would be Jesus. Jesus did not come to reinforce the ten commandments. He did not come to beat a dead horse but to make the dead *alive*. All mankind is dead on the inside without Christ. Jesus did not even judge those who heard His words and did not believe because He came to not judge the world but to save the world. God ultimately judges people based on whether they rejected Jesus and His message on the day of judgment (John 12:46-48). This is the only vital question and the question that will matter forever.

When Jesus saw sin and its terrible effects, He was moved with compassion because He knew without a good Shepherd, they were always going to be lost, harassed, and helpless—didn't matter if they were dignitaries or a woman working the streets (Matthew 9:36, NLT), they were all dead and were only capable of dead works of the flesh. Right after this, Jesus says to his disciples, "The harvest is great, but the workers are few. So, pray to the Lord who is in charge of the harvest; ask Him to send more workers into His fields" (Matthew 9:37-38, NLT).

The solution that Jesus proposed was to ask God for workers to declare the good news of the Kingdom. The problem was not the harvest (the lost people) or how sinful they were but the lack of workforce who truly believed that Jesus was the Savior who could save, set free, deliver and change people from the inside out by giving them a new nature. Everything else is a band-aid fix. We (the church) are the problem, not the lost world. God holds us accountable. It's time for us to declare that nations are washed by the blood of Jesus, and they shall be saved and agree with God's desire to save every soul. If we don't believe what Jesus has achieved is infinitely more impressive and powerful than Adam's sin, we will have very little to offer to a hurting world. The only one that can take us from death to life is Jesus! The only one who can give us a heart of flesh and a new nature is Jesus! God's greatest asset is people, and our greatest asset is Christ.

In the Old Testament, Noah was the first man to have found grace in the eyes of the Lord (Genesis 6:8). In Genesis 5:29 (AMP), "He named him Noah, saying, "This one shall bring us rest and comfort from our work and from the [dreadful] toil of our hands because of the ground which the LORD cursed." Noah's father, Lamech, named him Noah, which meant rest, repose, and peace and that he would bring rest, comfort, and relief instead of toil and agonizing work because of the curse. What a powerful name! This is a shadow of Jesus who came to give us rest and relief from toils and burdens that were part of the curse of sin.

Noah found undeserved kindness and favor from God, and because of God's grace upon him, he was able to live a just and righteous life. In Genesis 9, Noah, and his family (three sons: Shem, Ham, and Japheth) are restarting their lives after the flood. Noah plants a vineyard has one too many drinks, gets drunk, and becomes naked and uncovered in his tent. Noah's son, Ham, saw the nakedness of his father and told his two brothers outside. Ham saw the nakedness, talked about the nakedness without covering the nakedness.

Shem and Japheth, on the other hand, took a garment, laid it on both their shoulders and went backward and covered the nakedness of their father. Their faces were turned away, and they did not see their father's nakedness. Shem and Japheth chose not to see the nakedness or talk about the nakedness but instead covered the nakedness.

When Noah gets sober and heard what his younger son, Ham, had done to him, he cursed him to be a servant of servants. On the contrary, Noah pronounced blessings on Shem and Japheth for turning their faces and covering his nakedness (Genesis 9:20-27). Even though Noah was 100 percent wrong for getting drunk and losing his self-control, and exposing his nakedness, he was still a man under God's undeserved grace. Ham's attitude and behavior were contrary to the grace of God. What mattered is not Noah's nakedness but God's grace that covered his nakedness and mistakes. No one can uncover and expose what was covered under the grace of God. I believe this is a shadow of our new recreated life in Christ.

God's grace and mercy triumph judgment (James 2:13b). Noah places a heavy curse on Ham to be a servant to his brothers and instead blesses Shem by saying, "Blessed be the Lord, The God of Shem"—Noah blessed Shem to be the God of the one who chose to honor and celebrate God's grace. Over Japheth, Noah pronounced a blessing of enlargement and increase. God's grace (living dependent on God's undeserved favor and kindness instead of our works) is the source of all our blessing and what enlarges us and grows us from the inside out. It takes great humility to live dependent on God's grace, looking to Jesus instead of our works. We can only show undeserved grace to others to the extent we've understood God's grace and mercy over us.

We have been set free from the law of sin and death and placed under of the law of *life* in Christ Jesus (Romans 8:2)—that is full of grace and mercy. We have a "Ham epidemic" in the global church, and until we understand how merciful and gracious God has been to us, we truly cannot live free and won't be able to set others free as God intended. We won't live blessed or enlarged as we should in Christ. We will gossip and expose one another's nakedness, breeding envy, jealously, and compromise the spirit of unity and love, which are our power weapons that will draw the world to Jesus. "By this, everyone will know that you are my disciples if you love one another" (John 13:35, NIV). Without God's love that can only come from our new nature, we are simply noisy and bankrupt; it doesn't matter if we have a big ministry or a large bank account (1 Corinthians 13:1-3).

Because of Jesus, we have found such undeserved grace in God's eyes. His favor surrounds us like a shield (Psalm 5:12). We were all born naked, but in Christ, He has clothed us with the robe of righteousness. God's unmerited kindness covered our nakedness and put them all on Jesus, so unlike Shem and Japheth, God can look at us and no longer see our nakedness, so He doesn't have to walk backward like they did. The Father comes running to us. If it was true in the old covenant for Noah, how much more those who are in the new covenant under the blood of Jesus! Thank you, Jesus!

JESUS WHO IS MUCH MORE!

Make sure you are fully awake with a cup of coffee when reading this chapter☺—it is packed with powerful scriptures to anchor you in Christ. Check out these scriptures that have *much more* pointing to the *much more* Jesus has accomplished for us. Trust in Jesus's accomplishment for you and the resurrection power in you for your every situation. Because of Jesus, we shall be saved *much more*; we have access to a *much more* glorious way giving us great confidence; we will reign *much more* E like a King; we have *much more* life and have *much more* grace! Hallelujah!

- Therefore, since we are now justified (acquitted, made righteous, and brought into right relationship with God) by Christ's blood, *how much more* [certain is it that] we shall be saved by Him from the indignation and wrath of God.

  Romans 5:9 (AMPC)

- For if while we were enemies we were reconciled to God through the death of His Son, it is *much more* [certain], now that we are reconciled, that we shall be saved (daily delivered from sin's dominion) through His [resurrection] life.

  Romans 5:10 (AMPC)

- If you then, being evil, know how to give good gifts to your children, *how much more* will your Father who is in heaven give good things to those who ask Him!

  (Matthew 7:11 (NKJV)

- *How much more* shall the blood of Christ, who through the eternal Spirit offered Himself without spot to God, cleanse your conscience from dead works to serve the living God.

  (Hebrews 9:14, NKJV)

- If the old way, which brings condemnation, was glorious, *how much more* glorious is the new way, which makes us right with God! In fact, that first glory was not glorious at all compared with the overwhelming glory of the new way. So, if the old way, which has been replaced, was glorious, *how much more* glorious is the new, which remains forever! Since this new way gives us such confidence, we can be very bold.

  2 Corinthians 3:9-12 (NLT)

- For if because of one man's trespass (lapse, offense) death reigned through that one, *much more* surely will those who receive [God's] overflowing grace (unmerited favor) and the free gift of righteousness [putting them into right standing with Himself] reign as kings in life through the one Man Jesus Christ (the Messiah, the Anointed One).

  Romans 5:17 (AMPC)

- So, if you sinful people know how to give good gifts to your children, *how much more* will your heavenly Father give the Holy Spirit to those who ask him.

  Luke 11:13 (NLT)

- But the free gift is not like the offense. For if by the one man's offense many died, *much more* the grace of God and the gift by the grace of the one Man, Jesus Christ, abounded to many.

  Romans 5:15 (NKJV)

Amazingly powerful what Jesus has accomplished for us. We have nothing without Jesus, but in Him, we are incredibly blessed. To overcome this life, it is important to know what the sin of Adam left in you versus what Jesus has accomplished for you so you can take a hold of your new nature.

Through Adam	Through Christ Jesus
When Adam sinned, sin entered all of humanity (Romans 5:12).	Through Christ, God's glorious grace, gift of forgiveness, and gift of righteousness came to us and will always be greater than all of mankind's sins (Romans 5:15, 17). Jesus is able once and forever to save those who come to God through Him (Hebrews 7:25, NLT). With His own blood, Jesus entered the Most Holy Place once for all time and secured our redemption forever (Hebrews 9:12, NLT).

Adam's sin led to condemnation (blame, disapproval, denunciation) (Romans 5:16).	Because of Jesus's one act of righteousness, we were brought into a right relationship with God even though we are guilty of many sins and a new life for anyone who wants it (Romans 5:18). We are forever accepted in Christ—free from all condemnation (blame, disapproval) (Ephesians 1:6; Romans 8:1).
The sin of Adam caused death to rule (Romans 5:17).	We reign as a king in life through Christ by receiving God's wonderful grace and His gift of righteousness (Romans 5:17). We don't triumph over sin by beating ourselves up and asking for forgiveness repeatedly—it will keep us bound. To live in freedom, we partake of what Jesus freely gave us—yielding to His love, His peace, His joy, His glorious grace, and His free gift of righteousness every moment.
Because Adam disobeyed God, we all became sinners—irrelevant how big or how small our sins were (Romans 5:19).	Because of Jesus's perfect obedience to God, we were made righteous (Romans 5:19).
We were headed to eternal destruction.	We have eternal life through Jesus our Lord when we deserved hell (Romans 5:21).

I am spending some time on this since I am believing there are many of you who were raised in church and still struggling to overcome like I did. In my struggles to grow in Christ, I remember the Lord telling me, "See yourself in the post-resurrected Christ, not a pre-resurrection Christ."

If Christ hadn't been risen, our faith is vain, our preaching is useless, there is no gospel (no good news), there is no resurrection from the dead for us, Jesus is not the God who came in the flesh, Jesus would be a liar, there would be no hope, no peace, no favor/goodwill towards us, no salvation for mankind and we are still in our sins (1 Corinthians 15:14-17; John 2:18-19; Romans 1:4).

Jesus's horrific death would be voided if He hadn't resurrected from the dead, and we would be still in our sins (1 Corinthians 15:17). Christ died for each of us individually in our place, our old man (sinful and corrupted) was crucified with Christ, and when He was buried, our sinful old man individually was buried with Him, but if Jesus did not resurrect, we would not be raised to a new life. The resurrection of Jesus was the game changer!

> And because of Abraham's faith, God counted him as righteous. And when God counted him as righteous, it wasn't just for Abraham's benefit. It was recorded for our benefit, too, assuring us that God will also count us as righteous if we believe in Him, the one who raised Jesus our Lord from the dead. He was handed over to die because of our sins, and He was raised to life to make us right with God.
> Romans 4:22-25 (NLT)

The post-resurrected Christ is the one who is eternally qualified to make us right with God—it is the resurrection of Jesus that proved that He is indeed God incarnate and allowed us to be counted as righteous through Him.

It is only by Christ's resurrection that His righteousness could be imputed (assigned) to us. The gospel does not stop with our sins being put on Christ, but it is finished with His righteousness being imputed to us (2 Corinthians 5:21). Without Christ's resurrection in righteousness, we could never be justified (considered just and righteous) by faith (Romans 4:22-25). Below highlights, if you are living in a "pre-resurrection" mode or living in the post-resurrected Jesus who is highly exalted with a name above all names.

Pre-resurrection Christ (dead to sin, but not alive to God)	Post-resurrected Christ (dead to sin, alive to God in Christ Jesus)
You have confidence that Christ died for your sins, but you struggle to believe you are in right standing before God.	You believe Jesus's death and resurrection were the most important and powerful cosmic events that ever happened in history, and you completely trust in it—Jesus not only took your every individual sin but also transferred God's righteousness on to you.
You believe at the time of your salvation you were justified (just and righteous) by faith, but you seem to go back to your "own" works and self-righteousness instead of placing your faith in what Jesus did.	You believe you are justified by faith (Romans 5:1; 3:28). You started by faith, and you continue by faith trusting in the post-resurrected Christ.
Most of the time, you live aware of your past and present sins. You struggle to see how righteous you really are.	You live humbled by how righteous God made you to be in the post-resurrected Christ.
You live for the most part with feelings of guilt and with a reminder of your sins and an unclean consciousness-similar to what you would expect under the old covenant sacrifices (blood of	You live secure in your redemption because of the post-resurrected Jesus. You live with a clean conscious that has been purified of your sinful deeds. I believe you can only truly worship God (in

bulls and goats), which could not perfect or secure anyone (refer to Hebrews 9).

spirit and in truth) with a pure conscious that was given to us by the blood of Jesus (Hebrews 9:14); it is not by "our works" so we cannot take any credit for it. So, worship becomes all about Jesus not us! All the blessing, glory, wisdom, thanksgiving, honor, power, and might will only be to our God eternally (Revelation 7:12).

You operate under a spirit of love, power, and sound mind that was given to you in Christ Jesus (2 Timothy 1:7). You live in the reality that in the perfect love of God, there is no fear, for fear has to do with punishment (1 John 4:18), and Jesus was punished harshly to set you free once and for all.

Because you don't see yourself raised with Christ, your mind is not set above, and you end up focusing on the things of this earth (the temporal—things that are quickly fading away). You are prone to get choked by the cares of this world, the deceitfulness of riches and desires of this life (Mark 4:19).

You believe by faith that you were raised with the post-resurrected Christ, and you gravitate towards the things which are above (where Christ is) (Colossians 3:1-2).

You seek the kingdom of God and His righteousness and believe all things will be added to you (Matthew 6:33). You are free from not having to chase anything that God has promised will follow you (goodness and mercy) or be added to you. You live free of striving, envy and jealously because you know God will not withhold any good from you—not when He did not spare Jesus for you (Romans 8:32).

You strive in your own strength to live free from the power of sin, and you are not lit up on the inside through Christ.	You consider (reckon) yourself to be already dead to the power of sin and alive to God through Christ Jesus (Romans 6:11).
Much of your living is based on wrong feelings and emotions and less on God's word and by faith.	Because you believe you have been made righteous in Christ, you have confidence to live by faith (Galatians 3:11; Hebrews 10:38, Romans 1:17), not by your feelings or by sight. I particularly like the scriptures in Romans 1:17 where it basically says that God makes us right in His sight from faith for faith (from beginning to the end, from start to finish, it will be accomplished by faith), and the righteous ones will live by faith. Apostle Paul is, therefore, not ashamed of the gospel that has accomplished so much for us, for it is the power of God for salvation to everyone who believes, to the Jew first and also to the Greek (Romans 1:16). This is all too important since God has no delight in His righteous ones [the one justified by faith] when we drawback (shrink in fear) and no longer live by faith [respecting man's relationship to God and trusting Him] (Hebrews 10:38, AMP).
You live unaware that you are already complete in Christ. You live primarily validated by things other than Christ. You struggle to be something, be someone, instead of believing you already are a prized glorious inheritance.	You live complete in Christ—your bank account, your possessions, your position/titles, your children, your ministry, your spouse, your degrees, your family pedigree, your good or bad past does not complete you or feed your ego.

Other things and people seem to control you more than Christ.	You realize that all your blessings came from God and ultimately given to you to enjoy and accomplish God's purposes, but they don't have the power to complete you. You are complete, nothing lacking, and your life is hidden with Christ in God (Colossians 2:10; 3:3).
Most of your prayers are petition prayers—asking God to do things for you. You don't exercise your power and authority given to you by Jesus and believe it is only reserved for a small group of saints. You don't realize the same power that raised Jesus from the dead (resurrection power) is inside of you (Ephesians 1:19-20). You don't have the confidence to believe that whatever you bind on earth is bound in heaven and whatever you lose on earth is loosed in heaven (Matthew 18:18), again you believe this is only for a subset of believers.

You fast and pray to try to get God's attention as if He is distant from you, has forgotten you, and needs to be woken up from sleep.

You pray, but you don't experience peace since you don't have peace with God, to begin with. | You live increasingly confident in your heavenly Father. Your faith comes from your Father's reputation, His character strengths, and have learned to trust in His faithfulness, His ways, His love, and affections toward you.

You bring your requests to God with thanks and able to receive the peace of God that surpasses all understanding to guard your mind and heart in Christ Jesus (Philippians 4:6-7). You stay in peace because you have peace with God (Romans 5:1) and keep your eyes on Him.

You understand that Christ in you is the hope of glory (Colossians 1:27), you are a carrier of God's presence, and the resurrection power lives in you. You are confident in exercising the power and authority of Christ as the Holy Spirit directs you. You believe in God to establish you (2 Chronicles 20:20b). |

	You fast and pray primarily to draw near to God and to develop greater inner strength, and to live from the recreated new nature. You pray boldly from a place of rest knowing that you already have God's full attention, He already knows what you need, and everything will be given (added) to you since you are His heir, His glorious possession and co-heir of Christ, and in Christ, you have been brought to His fullness.
You struggle to believe you are a new creation and therefore, you do not occupy your seat in the heavenly realms in Christ Jesus. You see yourself in the old nature. You easily lose your peace, come under fear and anxious thoughts since you are not fully living seated next to Jesus and in Christ.	Because you believe you were raised from the dead when Jesus resurrected, you now live seated with Christ in the heavenly places (Ephesians 2:6). God did this so He can point to us as examples for eternity of the incredible wealth of His grace and kindness toward us, as shown in all He has done for us who are united with Christ Jesus (Ephesians 2:7). You live on the earth, but you think, work, minister and do life as if you were seated next to Jesus in the heavenly places. You don't easily come under anxiety or fear as you are seated near the King of glory. I believe this is similar to Psalm 91 promise to those who live in the shelter of the Most High and abide in the shadow of the almighty.

	You live in the heavenly places far above all rule and authority, power and dominion, and every name that is invoked, not only in the present age but also in the one to come (Ephesians 1:21). Seated in Christ, demonic weapons do not prosper in your mind.
Does not fully believe you are already holy and flawless before God—ends up living a life of striving with little transformation.	Believes you are already holy and flawless before God in the newly created nature (Colossians 1:22), and the Holy Spirit is working on transitioning you out of your old nature into the new nature by the renewing of your mind.

"For sin shall not have dominion over you, for you are not under law but under grace" (Romans 6:14, NKJV). Sin has less and less grip on you as you live under the freedom of God's grace. Our old nature only knows how to operate under law, but the new nature can only flourish under God's grace. In general terms, I believe there are only two laws— law of the spirit of *life* in Christ Jesus versus the law of *sin* and *death* (Romans 8:2). Jesus set us free once and for all from the law of sin and death—Broadly speaking, I see this category of "law" as simply "man's efforts" apart from Christ to produce a God fruit (fruit of the Holy Spirit). This is impossible!

You have died with Christ, and He has set you free from the spiritual powers of this world. So why do you keep on following the rules of the world, such as, "Don't handle! Don't taste! Don't touch!"? Such rules are mere human teachings about things that deteriorate as we use them.

> These rules may seem wise because they require strong devotion, pious self—denial, and severe bodily discipline. But they provide no help in conquering a person's evil desires.
>
> Colossians 2:20-23 (NLT)

> Realizing the fact that law is not made for a righteous person, but for those who are lawless and rebellious.
>
> 1 Timothy 1:9a (NASB)

Any law following or rule keepings will always produce sin and death in us because we empower the wrong nature (old dead nature). The more we try in our old nature, the more we will fail. We have been set free from the old nature to a brand-new nature to live by faith in the post-resurrected Jesus who will automatically produce His *life* in us. We need to learn to abide in Jesus (trusting, adhering, and relying on Him alone) to live in the new nature. God's grace (what Jesus has already accomplished and freely given to us) is what empowers the new nature—learn to accept His grace with wide-open arms even when you feel so undeserving to receive such a priceless gift. If you are led by the Spirit, you are not under law (Galatians 5:18) or under your efforts to produce godliness.

I believe the law was written on our hearts and into our minds (in our new nature) when we accepted Christ; God gave us a new heart and a new spirit (heart of flesh) that is now fully responsive to God's touch (Hebrews 8:10, Jeremiah 31:33, Ezekiel 36:26, Ezekiel 11:19). Amen!

> But this is the new covenant I will make
> with the people of Israel on that day, says
> the LORD: I will put my laws in their
> minds, and I will write them on their
> hearts. I will be their God, and they will
> be my people. And they will not need
> to teach their neighbors, nor will they
> need to teach their relatives, saying, "You
> should know the LORD." For everyone,
> from the least to the greatest, will know
> me already. And I will forgive their wick-
> edness, and I will never again remember
> their sins.
>
> Hebrews 8:10-12 (NLT)

I believe our new recreated nature is pre-programmed to live a life that is worthy and pleasing to God—it is built in us so we can be highly successful in our Christian walk. Our new nature carries God's instructions and comes with the ability to know God and have a wonderful, confident relationship with God with a vibrant heart towards Him. All is well and perfect in our new nature. The new nature, by default loves to submit to God, obey Him and can hear the Shepherd's voice clearly and follow Him and no other. Our new nature is like God—powerful, holy, filled with wisdom and insight. It is free from torment and perfected in His love. This is the nature that God is after—this is the nature He is trying to enlarge and grow within us. He already killed off the old nature, so God is not interested in keeping that old man in check but wants the old nature to be put off so the new can take over.

This built-in God nature in you can only be manifested by fully relying on God's efforts, not yours, believing that you are already in the post-resurrected Jesus to produce God-size transformation and fruit. This is living submitted to God and Jesus's accomplishments for God's built-in nature to take root in us!

"For the grace of God has appeared that offers salvation to all people. It teaches us to say "No" to ungodliness and worldly passions and to live self-controlled, upright, and godly lives in this present age" (Titus 2:11-12, NIV). Only God's glorious grace (free and undeserving) enables our built-in programmed new recreated nature to grow up so we can automatically say "No" to ungodliness and say "Yes" to godliness.

Colossians 2:6 (NLT) says, "And now, just as you accepted Christ Jesus as your Lord, you must continue to follow Him." We continue to walk out our sanctification just the same way we accepted Jesus—by faith and confidence in what Jesus has accomplished, trusting in His glorious grace—God in His brilliance made sure everything is dependent on His goodness, not ours, His qualification, not ours, His righteousness not ours. We would have been toast if it depended on us!

You follow Christ and "unfollow" you—"unfollow" your imaginations, your opinions, your feelings, your efforts, your toiling, your obedience, your goodness, your past, and your struggles. Because you are dead in Christ, if you follow your "dead self," you will not overcome, you will become frustrated, and it will keep you stuck.

The difference between man's efforts and trusting in God's efforts is highlighted in the birthing of Ishmael or Isaac, respectively. I think of birthing of Ishmael representing the "law"—where man is working while God is at rest to produce a temporary fix that results in great pain and strife versus Isaac as a representation of "grace"—where is God working and man is resting to produce a permanent covenant promise full of *life* in imperfect people.

When we live focused on ourselves, we empower the slave part of us (flesh; old nature) that was born of the physical descent (natural human attempts). This will always result in defeat. When we live focused on Jesus, we empower our inner recreated life (reborn from above) and become son of the free woman (supernatural). We cast out the bondwoman and her son (representing our flesh, our efforts) since only the son of the free woman that is supernaturally birthed (by God's efforts) can share the inheritance (Galatians 4:28-31).

In fact, in Genesis 16:9, the angel of the Lord tells Hagar, who ran away from Sarai because of how badly she was treated to, "Return to your mistress and submit to her." While we are living on this earth and in the flesh, we will always have to deal with our corrupt flesh, but it must always be submitted to the Spirit and not be our boss.

"So if the Son sets you free, you will be free indeed!" (John 8:36, ESV). Free of what? Free of first and foremost *"you"* (your old nature) and bound to Jesus in your new nature possessing *all* that He is. "For He made Him who knew no sin to be sin for us, that we might become the righteousness of God in Him" (2 Corinthians 5:21 NKJV). Every speck of our old nature with all its sinful inclination is already in Christ. Bible instructs us to work "out" our salvation (from the inside out—transition to the new recreated nature) with God's help (Philippians 2:12). We will struggle to do this successfully if we don't realize we have already become the righteousness of God with a built-in God nature allowing us free access to live abiding in Jesus. This is why in Galatians 5:22-23, where it talks about the nine fruit of the Spirit, it says against such things; there is no law. Our efforts (representing the law) simply won't produce any of the God fruits.

In my struggles, I remember the Lord telling me, "Learn to get the monkey off your back and on to Jesus." I believe this is true for our transformation as well as learning to completely unload our burdens and cares to Jesus, so we don't have to live anxious or worried. The latter isn't helping the situation and only makes things worse by not allowing room for God to work. I like the online Merriam-Webster's definition of "get the monkey off one's back": "to remove or solve a problem that has been difficult to get rid of or solve: to get rid of a problem or situation that makes one unhappy and that lasts for a long time." Whatever the problem or situation that is causing you to be restless, losing sleep over, or even a long-term addiction that you can't seem to get rid of—see that problem on Jesus's back and see yourself completely free in your new nature.

It's a journey where we will grasp for air with blows of the enemy as we learn to abide in Christ, but Jesus has already prevailed and overcome everything for us. The enemy is, at best, a headless serpent making a lot of noise and always trying to get in our face to make us live from our old nature. May you learn to *rest* in Jesus who *is much more* and in a God who always leads us in triumph in Christ!

YOUR CHOICE: TO ABIDE OR NOT TO ABIDE IN CHRIST

Jesus makes this bold statement in John 15:5 (NLT), "Yes, I am the vine; you are the branches. Those who remain in Me and I in them, will produce much fruit. For apart from Me, you can do nothing."

Our greatest blessing on earth is to live a life abiding in the Vine (united with Christ). We get to live in union with the most powerful, kindest, and humblest person in the cosmos. This means you get to partake in the life, power, wisdom, discernment, revelation, mind/attitude, the love, the compassion, the humility, the boldness, the discipline, the forgiveness and the motivation of our Lord Jesus Himself. Simply amazing that we are blessed with so much in Christ! We get to become partakers of His divine nature (2 Peter 1:4). God has lavished us with so much grace and spoiled us rotten in Christ!

This is where spiritual growth happens, great adventures with God, fruitfulness, and a truly fulfilled life. We become His witness, fragrance, and an epistle of Christ to be read (Isaiah 43:10; 2 Corinthians 2:14b; 3:3a). This is where I believe we come into Hebrews 4 rest of God prepared for all His precious children where we cease from our "own" works and work through Christ in our new nature.

God highlighted John 15 several years ago and probably is the most read chapter for me. John 15:7 (NKJV) makes this incredible "too good to be true" promise, "If you abide in Me, and My words abide in you, you will ask what you desire, and it shall be done for you." When you abide in Christ (from the new nature) and His words richly dwell in your heart, God backs you up, and you will see and experience things that others won't. It is a rich place of submission to Christ.

It's simple, we can do a lot of things without Christ, but the things that matter in the end and will produce lasting fruit will be the things that were done connected to Christ. It doesn't matter how small or big the task God calls you to. When all is said and done, the fire will test the quality of our work, and I believe only the work that we do united with Christ can withstand the fire, will remain forever and be richly rewarded because it was done on the right foundation (Jesus Christ) (1 Corinthians 3:11-15).

When you accepted Christ, He came into your heart, and He already lives in you, but you will decide how much of Jesus will be lived through you.

- It is no longer you living, but Christ living in you and through you (Galatians 2:20).
- On the outside, it is you working at the office, but it is not you (not working from your old nature) but Christ working through you (in union with your new nature).
- It is you speaking, but it is not you but Christ speaking through you.
- It is you praying, but it is not you but Christ praying heaven's will through you.

- It is you raising the children, but it is not you but God raising His children through you. You are raising His children for Him. You are not raising your children for Him or your children for yourself. God is infinitely more interested in your children because they belong to Him and for His purposes.
- Christ in you is the hope of glory, and He gets to manifest Himself in the physical realm through you.

I believe this is the most dreaded place for the devil. He will use anything to distract, hinder and discourage you but his end goal is to stop you from laying a hold of the things that God has already given freely to you in Christ and prepared for you to enter into.

I've grown to appreciate this scripture in 2 Timothy 2:20-21 (ESV):

> Now in a great house there are not only vessels of gold and silver but also of wood and clay, some for honorable use, some for dishonorable. Therefore, if anyone cleanses himself from what is dishonorable, he will be a vessel for honorable use, set apart as holy, useful to the master of the house, ready for every good work.

> "For many are called, but few are chosen" (Matthew 22:14).

We decide if we want to be "chosen" and what type of vessel we want to be; vessels of gold and silver successfully went through furnace of afflictions and were refined, unlike vessels of wood and clay (they went through much less process). God uses trials to transition us from our old nature to the new God nature with the goal of living this short life united with Christ. Tests and trials have a humbling effect on us, so our corrupted flesh gets a chance to die, and our inner man has an opportunity to become stronger, so we can be like an expensive special utensil set apart for God's special purposes. There will be greater humility knowing that you are only a vessel, an ordinary jar of clay privileged to carry the greatest treasure, and God chooses which vessel to use for what purpose. If He chooses someone else, you trust that they were better suited for that work than you are.

We raise kids, and the goal is to progressively get them on their two feet; the goal is independence, so they are emotionally, mentally, physically, and financially capable to function on their own. In God's upside-down Kingdom, we start fully independent of God but progress towards becoming fully dependent on Him. As the old nature gets crucified, the new nature that is righteous, holy, and wonderful starts to become the new reality. The more dependent you are in Christ, the greater your spiritual maturity and growth. God dismantles our independence which brings no real life, no lasting value to us or anyone else, and trains us to live completely abiding in Christ. This is where we become alive, and rivers of living water flow from us that have the power to change and shift things. We live a rich and satisfying life following His voice, being led to the good pastures, He has already prepared for us, and living in the safety, protection, comfort, and provisions of the sheepfold. John 10:9-10 (NLT), "Yes, I am the gate. Those who come in through me will be saved. They will come and go freely and will find good pastures. The thief's purpose is to steal and kill and destroy. My purpose is to give them a rich and satisfying life."

I believe some of us sadly die on the lawn of the Kingdom of God and never step our foot into God's house or come into the rooms of His house or sat at His table to experience the richness of all that He already prepared for us to partake of. We came to the kingdom with pride, anxiety, fear, self-righteousness, selfishness, envy, and jealously (that is exactly the expectation that we come in just as we are with our all baggage), but we cannot remain year after year, decade after decade dealing with the same issues. Something is wrong!

Your old nature (flesh) cannot abide in Christ. It doesn't matter how wonderful of a person you are—your old nature is so corrupt that it will always be hostile to God; it can never obey God and can never please God (Romans 8:7-8).

We were grafted into the Vine when we accepted Christ. Only our spirit man (recreated to be holy and righteous) is designed to live united with Christ, and the strength of your connection with Christ will be the level of transformation that you have allowed to happen in your mind (Romans 12:2). Greater the change in our thinking (renewal of our mind), the greater the connection and abiding in Christ. On the contrary, the lesser the renewal of the mind, the lesser the strength of your connection with Christ.

The place of abiding is where you mature and can discern God's perfect and acceptable will for your life. You will start bumping into it because you are connected to the *Great I Am*. There will not be confusion or fogginess in your spirit—decisions will be accompanied with supernatural peace and confidence and divine alignment. God's word truly starts to become a lamp to your feet and light to your path (Psalm 119:105). You become confident in taking one step at a time and comfortable with uncertainties or seeming lack of progress. You are okay with not knowing how, what, when, or why. You are energized to do what pleases God—it brings you joy and peace to do what God wants you to do. This becomes progressively easier as we grow in our union with Christ.

However, this is a fight of two completely opposing natures—on one side, there is your flesh, the enemy, and the world conforming you to keep living in the flesh (old nature) and give way to all its demands. On the other side, there is God our Father, Lord Jesus, the Holy Spirit, the Word of God, host of angels, and the great cloud of witnesses who have gone before us, cheering us on to fight the good fight and stay on the Vine (Christ). The only way to win is to learn to keep your mind focused on Jesus (fully believe, trust, and rely on Him), His promises, believing you are already victorious, and ignore your flesh/the logical mind, the devil, and the patterns of this world. "But you belong to God, my dear children. You have already won a victory over those people, because the Spirit who lives in you is greater than the spirit who lives in the world" (1 John 4:4, NLT).

All of us go through peaks and valleys, but life will be difficult than it needs to be where there is minimal to no renewing of the mind. You can count on your yoke to be challenging and burdens too heavy because you are lifting the weight on your own. Without real transformation within, we are simply not able to trust God or give Him our burdens or let Him fight our battles or even have faith in Him—we can say we trust God with our words, but it would not be the reality of our hearts.

I know well because I used to be one and don't want to ever go back. So, I can relate to the pain of not seeing answers to prayers for years, doing the right thing and not expecting to see the outcome you hope to see, going to church, serving at church, paying tithes but getting discouraged, disillusioned, and easily falling into the trap of whether God has forgotten you. This is a dangerous slow death of your spirit man, which is your most precious asset. This is a vulnerable place that the enemy takes full advantage of us, a place where we can be easily deceived, and he feeds us more lies, hoping we would not pursue God fully. Hebrews 2:1 (NIV), "We must pay the most careful attention, therefore, to what we have heard, so that we do not drift away."

We need to fully appreciate the reality that our old nature (human heart) is 100 percent in darkness—there is no light, no truth, and nothing good. This human heart of ours is full of pride, is selfish and envious, keeps every record of wrong, cannot trust, cannot persevere, it will always fail us, and we, in turn, will fail others. This is where we all begin our journey with God. The point is to develop a hatred for this old nature that Jesus already took upon Himself and a love for the new nature that is like Him.

A lot of us who came from good stable homes with a solid education, having good-paying jobs, and businesses have a harder time with true transformation because we have enough good things going for us and, in a way, able to survive without being transformed to be like Jesus. We have managed to live successfully with our dysfunctions and know how to live within the backdrop of our "dark" hearts. In most cases, we are not even aware of the condition of our inner life or able to diagnose what the problem is.

We aren't desperate to be transformed because it is not an imminent threat. To top it, if you came from a "performance" driven church culture, over time, you've successfully mastered the habits necessary to fit into church life and culture. You know what to say, how to say, when to say, how to act, how not to act, how to dress and say the right prayers. Since our appearance and reputation are more important than becoming like Jesus, we have a difficult time owning up to what's not working and receiving help from God and others. Some of you don't trust church folks because you got hurt by immature believers who gossiped, used things against you, and made matters worse. This is unfortunate. The safest place on earth should be the church—where we can be honest and transparent, where we receive healing for our brokenness and wounds. We should have such a love walk with God that we can challenge one other to live in greater transformation.

If you are of Southeast Asian descent like I am, the problem is confounded because it is not just about you; it's about your whole clan, their wellbeing, your children's future, and your family's reputation is on the line—it becomes easier to put on a mask, put some spiritual makeup and concealers and pretend your way through life than confront your giants. We fail to realize that while we are working hard to give a good future and the best education money can buy for our kids, the best gift any parent can give a child is a more Christ-like version of *you*. I believe a lot of times, the giants we fail to slay and defeat, have to be dealt by the next generation, and it slows down and hinders the purposes and plans of God in our family line. It's one of the reasons why the enemy fights so hard for us to be free from our old nature—because freedom (Christ) in you has a positive God-size impact not only on you but also on your generations as well.

The best legacy to pass on to our next generation is to defeat the giants of pride, insecurities, victim mindsets, addictions, emotional, mental, and sexual bondages, anxiety, and our life to point to the reality of Jesus. We should not accept that our natural human DNA has more power than our spiritual God DNA when it comes to our behavior and attitudes. That is undermining Jesus, the power of the cross and resurrection, and everything Christ went through to get us back to God. That is undermining the gospel, which is the power of God unto salvation—not just to get us to heaven but to get heaven into us.

You don't have to settle for what was given to you from past generations, by what happened to you, by the help of the Holy Spirit, you get to raise the bar of righteousness in Christ. I pray that you will get desperate enough, have a deep spiritual hunger to strive to live abiding in Christ and under the rest of God.

It is scary yet a beautiful and powerful place of abiding in Christ when we feel powerless, as darkness caves in when we don't have all the resources or answers, don't have what it takes to succeed and when all odds are against us. We were designed to be outnumbered and were created for impossible feats. We were meant to be weak and foolish in the natural, but strong, powerful, and more than conquerors in the Spirit. God's grace covers what we are not. For when we are weak, then we are strong (2 Corinthians 12:10). Such is the paradox of living in the God cycle under God's mighty hand and under God's undeserving grace.

You were designed to face and overcome the bears, the lions, the adders, the serpents, the Goliaths, the lion's den, fiery furnace, the Red Sea, Jericho, and Haman's plans. All challenges and obstacles must bow to Jesus in you. The enemy flees because of the presence of Jesus you carry. You were designed to shift atmospheres and environments through Christ. You are stronger and powerful than you know because of the greater ONE who lives inside of you.

As you live this momentary life in the God cycle (from Him, in Him, through Him, and for Him), I have no doubt that God will absolutely show up and show out in and through you infinitely beyond your greatest prayers, hopes or dreams!

APPENDIX

If you don't know this amazing Savior, Jesus Christ, please say the following simple prayer to invite Him into your heart. It will be the very best decision you ever make:

Dear God, I need you, and I come just as I am. I am sorry for my sins and the way I have lived. I receive Jesus as my Savior and Lord. I believe that Jesus died for my mistakes and failures. He rose from the dead and is alive today. I receive a new start in Jesus by becoming a new creation with a new nature. I trust in what Jesus has already done for me. I believe I am saved. Thank you for forgiving me, saving me, and giving me eternal life in you. Amen.

Contact Info

You may contact Judy Pattassery at Godcyclelife@gmail.com.

CPSIA information can be obtained
at www.ICGtesting.com
Printed in the USA
FSHW010339070721
82886FS